I0013147

TABLE OF CONTENTS

WEB MONEY

TIPS, TRICKS AND TECHNOLOGY TO START WEB BUSINESS

First of all I would like to thank all the girls who said no to me, and Iam single since a very long time, being single allowed me lot of time to focus on new things and new ideas, and allowed me time for learning, experimenting

You don't need to buy cow to have milk, you can directly buy milk.

--Albert Einstein ☺ ☺

Initially when I published this book, I thought to tell you just one technique to make money, by starting a website, but now I have added all different ways you can make money online, technique to make money just from website is still there, but I have also added other ways

Internet has made more millionaires in last 5 years than past 50 years combined, web has opened new opportunities', to make millions you need to affect millions, that's the secret of large wealth, website expose your business to the whole planet, any person on this planet can be your customer

Here in this eBook, I will be talking about technology and about ways to make money via website, I have also added many other ways to make money online, this book will be frequently updated; any new ideas about making money online will be added.

I want my eBook to be best seller, that's why iam adding lot of useful information in this book and also keeping the price lowest.

I will also tell you where you can find complete free source code to start website, websites are coded by me, which you can download and start your website, you can use them whatever way you want, modify it and use it for commercial use but don't sell it, without paying me first ☺

There are 1000s of ways to make money online and new ways to make money online spring up every day; it's like "so many girls and so little time"

This book is basically about how you can start a website and make money from it, but I have also added other ways to make money online, it will just help you more.

This is not ghost script, I have not paid any one to write this book, I have written it myself with all the experience I have in web technologies and making money doing it, I want you to read all of my book, and give your honest opinion, you can join our website and also suggest me how to improve the product and add other benefits.

HOW MONEY IS MADE, WHEN MOST OF SERVICES ARE FREE ON INTERNET

Internet giant Google, Facebook don't charge

anything for services, yet make billions of dollars profit

It's because you the user are there products which they sell it to advertisers, Google keeps track of your every search, your ad clicks and they know what you are looking for, Google knows you better than you know about yourself, which helps them show ads relevant to what you are looking for.

Data belongs to the collector, since you have voluntarily given your data to these companies to use their free services, its theirs now; they use your data to serve you better, understand you better and serves advertisements which are more targeted to you.

Everything about you, your likes, dislikes and searches, they know where you go, your habits, everything is stored in big data and algorithms can easily categorize you.

Google gave android for free, it is the most used operating system in mobile phones, Google is swimming in money, app developers have to pay Google to get there app listed in Google play, plus they get 30% for the every app that gets sale. They are currently making 30-60 billion dollars every year just from android, so free is never free there is a catch in it.

Amazon.com is making whooping money, its making 5-6 million per day selling just eBooks for kindle in United States. That's a lot of money just from eBooks in one country, amazon has lot of innovative products and I praise them for their innovation, but many of their good services are only available in United States, I hope they are available for whole planet

If you want to know about their innovation, just search for "Amazon Echo" in YouTube, I guess amazon will surpass Google, the kind of innovation they are doing is
mind blowing, Google has got itself into arms and ammunition so they might fall short for innovating for everyday people, since they are busy in military.

There is new technology coming up inmobi, which will target your mobile with ads which are very relevant to you, mobile gives your location wherever you go, it has sensors to detect temperature, blood pressure
don't get surprised all of a sudden, if you sees Ads for Air conditioner when the temperature around you gets too hot, your mobile detected it and communicated it.

Instagaram never made a single rupee, but yet it was purchased by Facebook for 2 billion dollars, and whatsapp was purchased for 20 billion dollars, it is said that they will use user's photos for advertisements, which so far they haven't done; it may be used for facial recognition biometric scanning

Google glass had that feature, if you look at some person with Google glass, it will show up his name from Google+ profile, it was very dangerous for privacy so Google removed it.

Edward J. Snowden Revealed

The agency intercepts "millions of images per day" — including about 55,000 "facial recognition quality images" — which translate into "tremendous untapped potential," according to 2011 documents obtained from the former agency contractor.

They do something about images; they use it for facial recognition, they know every person by name that's for sure.

It might be that Mark Zuckerberg be the biggest CIA Agent.

Government uses this data to track criminals, track terrorists. Facebook has saved CIA hours of work.

Mark Zuckerberg was also Awarded CIA Surveillance Medal

In this book, I will explain you, how you can start your own web business with little required skill, one useful website, its design and sticky strategy, how to make visitors come again and again. What technology to use, how you will make money

Although there are many services you can start on your own, but I will explain you the easiest 1 any can start, without much resources, I assume that you are a single individual, with some technical and programming skills, but with less money and wants to do something

Services like Online Ticketing, ecommerce, online grocery store, are not that easy to start, since it will require you to have staff and lot of money.

I will teach you how to start a basic useful website, which won't require you to hire staff and you can earn money by showing Google AdSense ads

I will also tell you technique where you can convert your website into mobile App

I will give you names and little info about how some people are making millions via internet and few other techniques where money can be made

I will also give you link to source code, which you can use and start your website

I also have a website for support http://www.websolutionsforum.com/

Where issues can be discussed and also source code will be given to premium members.

The people who purchase my eBook and give honest reviews to my eBook on amazon, will be given premium account, no payment required, he will be able to download the source code of websites which we are using.

I will be giving fully functional dating site coded in asp.net mvc, C# and Mongodb and also dating website built in meteor.

See here iam using Mongodb for database not SQL Server, SQL Server cannot be used as database for a large website with high traffic, product is highly scalable even if millions register and visits everyday no problem.

Those software worth well over $3000, but my eBook purchaser will get it for free.

We are also coding dating website in nodejs, which will be given for free to our eBook buyers

I have a team who programs, I myself is a programmer

We do not provide technical support on individual level, if there is an error you can report it, software is well tested and used, personal level support is not possible, customization at personal level not possible, since we already are loaded with work.

NEW WAVE OF ADVERTISING

You must have noticed whenever you look at some product, that product ad seems to follow you, even when you visit other website, these ads seem always there, Ads staring right into your eyes, this may look creepy
this type of advertising is called Re-marketing or behavioral targeting ads

This started as a way to encourage shoppers to come back to an e-commerce site when they abandoned an online shopping cart has now turned into a system that tries to stay in front of website visitors wherever they go

The reason that an advertiser seems to be following you around is because they placed a cookie on your computer when you were visiting their site. The use of cookies (small text files) that help advertisers track your online behavior, and re-marketing companies are just the latest to make use of them and add more profits.

Targeted advertising can be more useful to us as consumers, but it can also get annoying, especially if we have already bought the product.

For example
if you visit amazon.com and searched asp.net books, and you viewed a particular asp.net book, then left it alone or purchased it, and then all of a sudden you will start to notice that Asp.net Book which you just saw, will be shown in Google ads, Facebook ads, you might wonder how the hell they know, you were looking into this book, no matter which

website you visit that ad will show up, it is so relevant that you might sometimes find it too creepy

Ad networks logic is that you were just about to make purchase of this book, and so they follow you to remind you to purchase. But they also show that same product ad even if you had already purchased that product, which is wrong.

Google added few more millions to their profits just by using this technique

ABOUT ME

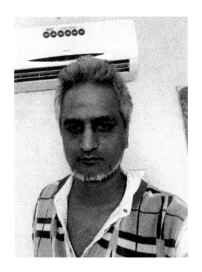

I am Amin b Nagpure, web developer and web marketer, made lot of money building web systems which work

You can follow me
http://www.aminnagpure.com

Iam also director of software company

It's not like since I was a little boy, I wanted be an affiliate marketer, my career just happened to me, when I was born there was no internet and web, I got into programming since I was unemployed for so long, that doing programming seemed to be only way to get job or making money.

Iam a programmer, web developer skilled in asp, asp.net, meteor, node, sql server, Mongodb.

I thank to internet for the all things I got from it, free source code, tutorials and tons of free information, internet also gave me my first job and my current business.

If you are programmer, it makes easy for you to start web business, since you are already aware of the things required for doing it.

Even if you are not a programmer, I will narrow down your learning curve, so that you only learn things which are most required.

In today's highly competitive market, you have to be technically skilled to be able to make unique system which works, you will have to change it from time to time, you can hire good programmers, you need to understand programming at least good enough, to know what is possible and whom to hire. Elance and freelance won't work much.

If you do not have technical skills, programmers might take advantage of you, by citing technical reasons which you don't understand, like my graphic designer used to give me technical reasons regarding video making, since I was not aware of things needed for video making, don't let them fool you.

Unless you are Steve jobs, who can hire great engineers without himself being an engineer, having good enough technical skills will help you hiring the right programmer to do your job.

I will teach you, what technology to use, marketing techniques and ways to make money from websites
Upcoming technologies and upcoming ways to make money.

EMERGING TRENDS

Technology have bought changes in human society, like invention of wheel, fire, agriculture, industrial revolution, current information age, all are actually technological changes.

This is information Age, anyone can be expert on any subject, and all the information is available on the internet all the time.

Spy gadgets are easily available for any one, that's why there are so many Sting Operations.

Understand the wave, so that you can ride it.

Connectivity has made learning very easy, if you want to learn kungfu(snake fist style), you may not find the tutor in your area, but online you can find step by step tutorials for it, there are paid and free tutorials available, there is also mobile app to train martial arts, exercises.

If anyone wants to learn how to sing, he can do so, there are 1000s of individuals offering singing courses, rap courses, guitar lessons, basuri lessons, dancing courses.

I myself have taken "How To Rap" classes online, it is cheap and expert teach you.

You can learn programming from the experts online, that's why local coaching classes business, is down.

Old jobs are quickly getting absolute, if we don't update ourselves or change according to the needs, and we can be absolute, worthless, and unemployable

Change gives rise to new opportunities, that's where we can click; we can fill the vacuum which change has created.

Change can also be very bad for well establish business, which are slow to adapt or two big to implement changes, this is where startups have advantage, they are young, aggressive, innovative, they have very less operating cost almost nothing to loose, and can quickly become millionaires when the opportunity strikes, you must have heard lot of these kinds of stories

I myself has changed a lot in so many years, started career as vb programmer, and then shifted to asp, then asp.net, now nodejs and meteor.

I had no choice but to learn new technologies to get more salary and be in demand.

Local taxis are slowly dying, because of ola cabs and uber

Local shop keepers have hard time selling products, because the same product is available at a very cheap rate online. clothes, shoes, mobiles are cheaply available online, shop keepers have to pay rent, plus they have to pay state and local tax, making

their goods very costly,
you can easily see they hardly make money,
their money is always invested in unsold stock.

I have seen one authorized shopkeeper of TITAN watches, he told me that he has over Rs20 lakhs invested in the watches stock, he is loosing interest on that money, if he had kept the same money in the bank, he could have earned around 2 lakh per anum interest, without doing anything. Or else he could have used that money in other productive purposes.

Somebody needs to tell that old fellow, that nobody buys watches now, they are absolute

I have also seen shops at malls selling VADA PAV, burgers, sandwiches, the rent in mall and operating cost is so high, that they can hardly make profit doing it. Lot of this type of food stalls get closed within a year.

Websites on the other hand are low maintenance, and has larger reach.

Websites can have a large variety of clothes, shoes online, because website is not limited by physical space while shops are limited to physical space, there is a limit to stock shopkeeper can keep

Even drugs, guns and hitmans are available online, for that you need to use TOR to surf these hidden sites; those websites can only be accessed by TOR.

Lot of opportunities are available in emerging technologies, like big data (lot of jobs available in big data, people are just not available)

Opportunities are there in web technologies, mobile technologies, internet TV

Keep an eye on TOR, Bit coin, and Dark Coin

Keep an eye on Decentralized computing and block chain technology, It seems future will be decentralized.

Now it is very easy to track everyone at all the time, because he/she carries cell phone, which constantly advertise its location

Criminals who running away from police can be easily tracked, because they have tracker in their pocket that is their mobile phone, which continuously shouts about his location

Now almost every mobile has speech recognition capability, if you say "CALL MOM", your mobile will call your mom.

World is coming closer now, everybody sharing ideas, taking photos, constantly updating their status, sharing selfies. too much information to digest, information on any subject is available for free and in large scale, anyone can be expert in any subject, if he just has pc and internet connection, or just a mobile phone, IIN the idea ad, the concept is real. We can be in touch with our friends all the time, and can also make new friends worldwide
Via what sup , Facebook or any other app

I believe most people could cure any disease just with Pub Med database research in about a month! No kidding, I myself has found lot of solutions for my common ailments, doctors are simply not able to fix it, but internet can

Here is the url
http://www.ncbi.nlm.nih.gov/pubmed

You know about "yeast infection" on your private part, it is actually caused by bad stomach, if you drink too much beer, sugar, that causes yeast infection, that is actually stomach problem but doctors will give you ointment, which might aggravate your problem, it is very common ailment, but doctor has no cure for it, I found a way for it from the internet. So many things doctor know are wrong. Skin infections are mostly caused by free flowing sugars in the blood, acidity, lack of vitamins but doctors will always give you ointment for that.

Anti-biotic is a bad medicine since it also kills the good bacteria, but still it is used, there is a whole new approach coming up to treat disease, it's a way having more good bacteria to counter bad bacteria, not to kill every one. Current method is to drop "Nuclear Bomb" (Anti Biotic) to kill every bacterium you have.

I can have whole chapter about doctors wrong medicine and the way they approach an issue.

Pesticide and fertilizers have damaged the soil by killing the life giving bacteria, in order to kill bad bacteria they are also killing good bacteria, drop nuclear bomb kill them all. There is a new method of farming which society must encourage farmers to do that is "Shiv Yog" farming method. Search on Google

Mobile phone will be smarter, will be our AIs, mobiles can help us to remember things, using reminders

M-PESA

Salute to Kenyans, they are the first whose 100% population is using mobile phones for payments, iam from India a lot advance country than Kenya, but I still use paper money, but Kenyans are using mobile phone and that too without using smart phones, people there are poor but they have proved to be smarter. Scarcity of resources sometimes leads to smarter solutions. M-pesa is in India, but the bank charges are too high for anyone to use it.

VANISHING DICTATORS

World is moving towards decentralization, that is there is no leader for an organization, everybody does their own part. Current system is centralized, where authority decides what everybody should do. Do search on YouTube for "blockchain" method and "decentralization"

Democracy will be established everywhere, even in Middle East countries and North Korea, they won't be able to suppress there people for a long now.

As social networking grows, people are well informed, no paid media, fake news, because people exchange information with each other dictators will have hard time keeping control.

Look what Facebook and twitter had done to oppressive regimes of Muhammad Hosni El Sayed Mubarak, Egyptian President.

Oppressive leader Muammar Gaddafi gone, dead
Bashar al-Assad Syrian president will be gone soon,
Saudi Royals will go soon, but USA is protecting them, they are very restrictive and

oppressive regime, which can give death punishment for simple anti govt tweet or comment

Only Middle East, and North Korea still has dictatorship, because the information there public receives is filtered by their government, tailored with added flavor's to suit the government.

In North Korea There are loud speakers on the streets, near houses, where dictators can spread their propaganda messages right into the ears of its citizens, this is very controlled oppressive regime, no freedom of speech or expression, one has to watch out for his words.

Once the people in North Korea realize that they are not treated as humans but pigs, they will rise up against this ping-pong dictator of their country.

I really feel sorry for people of North Korea, Middle East world is moving forward doing innovations and they are misinformed, and still worshiping there wrong god like leaders.

I just cannot imagine living in such countries without basic freedom and freedom of speech.

Middle East countries are blinded by their religion, and ruling party is taking advantage of it, they still follow 1400 yr. old rule. Their religion controls what they eat, what they do, what they are supposed to do.

That's why people don't lineup to be a citizen of Saudi Arabia; people from there are running away to other countries, they are scared of sharia law. Too many strict laws are bad for peaceful life, people hate strict laws it worries you all the time, and give too much power to police who use it to make more money.

I think West is unable to explain these middle east people merits of democracy and free speech, current Syrian rebels and ISIS almost have same ideology, none of them is supporter of democracy, they just wants there dictatorship

Obama Administration wanted to ouster butcher Assad and wanted to establish democracy in Syria, which is a good thing to do, but in doing so they made a mistake of supporting wrong people, jihadis which are even more butcher than Assad.

United States must end all ties with Saudi Arabia, a leader of democracy and free speech supporting radicals who believes in strict sharia law implementation, not even allow there women to vote, not allow there women to drive, forces women to cover their body from head to toe, and such oppressive regime is friends of united states.

A country which can send satellites beyond solar system, send man on the moon, take photographs and weather reports from all the planets and moon in the solar system, can make Hubble telescope, can take photographs of distant galaxies, can make good Hollywood movies like "Iron Man", but cannot make cars which can be driven on electricity or some other form of energy, they got to beg Saudis for oil, and support them in doing wrong things, like killing its own citizens, suppressing there freedoms and expressions.

United States is also providing intelligence data to Saudis royal family, providing advance weaponry, helping as much as they can to oppress people, only reason Saudis royal family still in office is American weaponry and intelligence. How come a super power like America so helpless, are there president on Saudis payroll.

No matter how hard they try sooner or later they will be and should be replaced by democracy

Social media fuelled anti-govt movement even in India, movement against corruption, India is democracy but corruption is high, anti-corruption movement got wide spread support due to social networking and Anna Hazare and Arvind Kejriwal emerged as new heroes

Twitter, Facebook, Google can be blocked, can be regulated by the government but there is also a decentralized app like twitter, which cannot be blocked, it's called TRSST.

http://www.trsst.com/

More sharing and more information will introduce new ideas and they will ask for change

Dictators are already very afraid of the internet and social media. They try censorship which is not in their full control.

Saudis royal family is also very worried

ROBOTS

Drones /robots will be the future, available for everybody, there is an open source robot technology

http://www.ros.org/

Ros means Robots operating systems

It is open source software libraries, which can help build you robots, it is an interesting technology, but has a high learning curve;

anyone can learn robot programming, make robots.

Drones are easily available for public to buy online, anyone can use them for spying, it is foreseen that terror organization like al-Qaida, Islamic state will use them for their suicide bombing mission, of course suicide bombers will miss there chance of meeting 72 virgins.

3D PRINTERS

3D printing or additive manufacturing is a process of making three dimensional solid objects from a digital file. The creation of a 3D printed object is achieved using additive processes. In an additive process an object is created by laying down successive layers of material until the entire object is created. Each of these layers can be seen as a thinly sliced horizontal cross-section of the eventual object.

Any object can be made with precise, minute details with 3D printers, Guns can be made with little efforts, cars can be made with unique design, and future of 3D printers is very promising

You should follow 3D Printing blogs, websites and Facebook pages, even if you are not into manufacturing; there is definitely an opportunity here.

Learn more about 3D printing
http://3dprinting.com/

3D Printing will automate production of spare parts or any other object.

There are people making money selling 3D printed objects, either they provide 3D printing service or print 3D printed objects and sell it on ebay.

These 2 websites below can help

https://www.sculpteo.com/en/

http://www.shapeways.com/marketplace/

join them to get idea about 3D printing industry and what it is.

CRIME CONVICTING
Indian state of Maharashtra convicted a woman of killing her ex-fiance, citing as proof

an EEG scan showing "experiential knowledge" of the crime.

When investigators hooked her up to an EEG and read aloud facts of the crime, however, software interpreting the electrical impulses in her brain told a story. "The relevant nooks of her brain where memories are thought to be stored buzzed when the crime was recounted."

This is horrifying for the crime; criminals have memories of the crime, which can be scanned, criminals will have hard time, hiding their crime, or they will have to have technology of "Men in Black", which can wipe out memories of crime.

VIDEO GAMES

There is also a big opportunity in video games, and lot of entrepreneur's have already made

millions from it.
For ex Zynga.

Owner of Zynga Mark Pincus made millions, leveraging Facebook social network to market its games. Now the relationship between Facebook and Zynga relationship is bit strained, Facebook being too greedy asking for more share in revenue from Zynga games, Facebook has restricted Zynga activities, but Zynga has other options too, it might tie up with yahoo, Gmail and let yahoo and Gmail users directly use Zynga games.

There is lot of money in video games, video game industry is said to be bigger than movie industry.

Nobody plays old way chess and carom, who has the time for that, and we need to find partner to play it, but in online games, playing partners are easily available, and there are huge variety of games, it is more exciting than chess and carom.

Building video games is not that hard, you can build video games with just html5 and

JavaScript. And with "Webrtc" technology, you can build network games

Here is the link for building network video games with Webrtc

https://github.com/agilityfeat/memory-webrtc-data-channel

Links for developing video games using JavaScript

http://craftyjs.com/

http://phaser.io/

For a bigger list
https://html5gameengine.com/

If you love video games and have lot of time, you can very well build your own video games.

This is new era for video games, no need for console games tools like Xbox. Games can be played on computer, and mobile phones. Video games Market is much bigger now, with open source tools and technology making video game has become easy.

WHAT YOU NEED TO BE TO START A WEBSITE

You need to be programmer yourself at least some basic skills, because finding and hiring talented people who can do your work will be difficult, and you won't be able to hire the right people, unless you understand technologies properly.

Paying for programmers will be costly, because your ideas may fail, skilled programmers are costly, you will have to judge programmer's capability, which will be difficult, if you don't understand it.

So go learn coding, learn at least enough to hire the right person, I will mention what technologies to learn in this book

Web administration skill, database skills and web coding skills are required

Gone are the days, earn money without working, make tons of money just by starting a website or a blog and make money by showing

Google ads, there are just too many people now in it, and every day new technologies and new app spring up. It's a competitive market now, because it has lot of money in it.

SO MANY GIRLS AND SO LITTLE TIME ☺

I will reduce your learning curve here, just learn JavaScript, html5 and CSS, it will take at most 2 days to learn html, even if you have never heard about HTML before, for CSS it will take 2 more days, and for JavaScript might take up to 7 days, even if you don't know programming.

So total around 10-12 days, you have to spend learning to be good enough to be web developer

Gmail was developed in JavaScript, and it was the first to be the real time email service. With JavaScript you can make real time Apps with ease.

GOAL OF THIS BOOK, WHAT YOU WILL ACHIEVE

After reading this eBook you will be able to understand web and how to make money from it. If you are non-technical person and could not understand some context in this eBook, it will still narrow down your search, you can always Google and learn more about it

I will show you what you can build easily and how to design it to make it more sticky, how to market it, there are numerous ways to make money on the internet, but we will make money by making dating website, dating website has lot of demand, people register on dating sites, even when they are married and have steady partners

I will tell you design strategy to make it more useful and sticky, marketing strategy

I will help you find motivation, by referring some individuals who have made it, made lot of millions from their websites and their internet skills

I have added other ways to make money online, so you can benefit more.

INSANE MONEY MAKERS

I will give info about few awesome money makers with link to their blog and profiles; you should follow them, to get ideas

Google loves blog, especially word press blogs, lot of people made insane money just by starting a word press blog, Google prefers blog in their search results and so these guys' made money automatically, insane money

When people are searching in Google, they are searching for information so Google drives them to blogs, People like to read blogs, because they want honest review, judgments not the sales pitch

NEIL PATEL

Neil Patel used to make over $10,000 per day by promoting adware/spyware removal programs,
and getting commissions from there sales, he just used to put advertise in Google AdWords, direct linking to the affiliate program product, users who used to search for spyware/adware removal programs would see his ads, click on

it and buy it, for every $10 spent on AdWords advertising he was making over $100, quite a lucky guy,

He is well known on internet.
I don't think he is making lot of money now; I follow him and he tells me, he works 10 hours every day even on weekends

Google disallows direct linking to affiliate programs, this trick won't work now, and his good old days are over now

His websites are

http://neilpatel.com/
http://www.quicksprout.com/

I don't think he is of any use now, since he got into it just by pure luck and made way too much money, it is a technical field now, he should have learned the technology by now, he is not a programmer, he is working hard on marketing skills and there are quiet a followers for him.

COURTNEY ROSEN

She is the owner of
http://www.ehow.com

purpose of ehow.com
Whether you need to fix, build, create or learn, eHow gives you practical solutions to the problems life throws at you. We empower you to efficiently solve each new challenge and make your life better and easier.
Worth of ehow.com is 151 million dollars, it makes around $50,000-$60,000 every day

Astounding for a blog, I told you Google loves WordPress blog; this is insane money for a simple blog with no technical skills at all

PETE CASHMORE

owner of

http://www.mashable.com/

His website is about news, stories and basic media stuff
its worth over $763 million, earning almost $ 157,798 / day just from AdSense

KEVIN ROSE

Owner of
http://www.digg.com/

It's just a news source blog, built in
WordPress, they share most talked about and
interesting stories
digg is valued around $150 million, and its
AdSense revenue per day is around $50,000.

SHAWN HOGAN

He is the owner of
http://www.digitalpoint.com
a very old site, it had AdSense ads earlier, but
now it seems they run their own ad system

Its website worth is around $46 million

He is also known for his famous incident with
eBay, he seemed to have looted ebay.com
with $28 million, by frauding there affiliate
program using cookie seeding technique

MICHAEL ARRINGTON

Owner of
http://techcrunch.com/

His blog worth massive $559 million
his AdSense revenue is around $60,000 per
day

PEREZ HILTON

Owner of
http://perezhilton.com/

Hollywood gossip and news blog
worth around $80 million, his website makes
around $30,000 per day

MARKUS FRIND

He created

http://www.pof.com

This guy has made a dating website to practice asp.net with sql server; it was hit in no time. He used newspaper advertisement to promote his website; his site soon started receiving lot of registration from Canada and later USA

A free online dating website
he earns over $20,000 per day just from

AdSense, and also makes ton of money from other affiliate programs

His success is from using algorithm to match profiles and by asking them to fill some answers to tricky questions

Not too bad for Asp.net and sql practice.
He keeps a low profile and not much available on social media

AMIT BHAWANI

His website

http://www.amitbhawani.com/

I had seen over 2 million G+ followers for this guy, now it's not visible, maybe he has hidden it

https://plus.google.com/102865818257357276162/about?rel=author

https://www.facebook.com/amitbhawani

This guy has a blog, where he started sharing internet tips, mobile tips and all tech related stuff, earns good money by showing AdSense ads, around $40,000 per month.

Basically now people search for review for products before buying them, like whenever someone wants to buy mobile, they search about it on the internet to know its positive and negative information, that's where his blog got lot of hits, because he was reviewing almost every mobile

Google prefers word press blog in search engine, and his blog got lot of hits

SHARDHA SHARMA

Shardha sharma's blog
http://www.YourStory.com

It is India's top media platform for the entrepreneurs, dedicated to the passionately championing & promoting entrepreneurial ecosystem in India. She earns around $40,000 per month, just by showing AdSense ads.

JEREMY SHOEMAKER

This guy made a ringtone website, converting songs into mobile ringtone, it was a hit in no time; you will find his photo allover on the internet with $132,994.97 check, he also has an audio book about him on audible.com and he used to host a radio show on http://www2.webmasterradio.fm/

His website is
http://www.shoemoney.com/

Now he seems to tutor people on how to make money.

AMIT AGARWAL

This guy used to do job in software co., one fine day he decided to leave his job, and started blogging; he soon had a large following and was able to make over $50,000+ every month from just a simple WordPress blog

http://www.labnol.org/

I have seen large following on his G+ profile, over 2.5 million, but now he has hidden the followers.
Almost no investment, works from home, writes a blog post once or twice a week and makes ton of money.

I told you Google loves WordPress blog.

PANKAJ AGARWAL

Owner of
http://www.clickindia.com

A classified website, earns around $20,000 per month from this simple website, classified website source code is freely available on the internet, you can download that and start your own classified website, it is little bit technical, but basic level programmer can do it.

SRINIVAS TAMADA

This guy is a programmer, and shares tips, tricks and source code on his website; he has his own Lamborghini, all programming money, his website is all about php, Ajax and website related stuff http://www.9lessons.info/, earns around $10,000 per month AdSense income, he also sells social networking script, like Facebook

You can follow him
https://www.facebook.com/srinivas.tamada

https://plus.google.com/+SrinivasTamada

His website

http://www.9lessons.info/

HONGKIAT LIM

His website
http://www.hongkiat.com/

His blog is about, web development, web design, templates, mostly all web related stuff.

He makes around $50,000 per month in AdSense.
His blog is worth around $86 million.

JACK HERRICK

His website
http://www.wikihow.com/

His website helps people, learn to do many things, in doing so; he makes over $350,000 per month from AdSense ads.

His website is worth massive $883 million.

KEVIN P RYAN

His website
http://www.businessinsider.com

Its website is about business and events, he makes around $200,000 per month, his website is worth massive $832 million.

Arun Prabhudesai

His website

http://trak.in/

His blog is about technology, he makes around $12000 per month in AdSense. His website is worth around $2 million, Quite good.

Jaspal Singh

His website
http://savedelete.com/

his blog is about technology, mobile phones. He makes around $7000 per month in AdSense. And his blog is worth around $100,000.

As you can see most high income bloggers are tech bloggers, giving tips, tricks and advice about technology.

ONLINE MLM SCHEMES

Robert Kioski a financial guru, expert in teaching how to make money and be rich the author of famous book "Rich Dad and Poor Dad", he wrote this book in 1999 and it still manages to sale lot of copies even today.

He has sold well over 26 million copies of that book.

You can find more about him on youtube.com

He recommends MLM marketing to get rich quick, because to start a business you need a product and also a marketing technique, which mlm schemes give you.

I have seen lavish life styles of these mlm marketers, they just flaunt their wealth to attract more people into their system, seeing such a lavish life style people follow them and ask them how can they make such an insane amount of money, basically lure of easy money attract people and people invest into it, but very few ppl manages to make money out of it.

I myself had joined 3-4 MLM programs, stayed there for 2-3 months just to check, understand them, check there marketing techniques, if you can convince someone to buy sheet and actually make him pay for it, that's a talent. But I didn't like the idea of making money by selling pyramid schemes, in India mlm is considered as scam and lot of people got arrested doing it. People avoid you, if they know that you have some mlm program in your mind, advertising mlm program is difficult, Facebook, Google bans it, even YouTube videos were removed if your video is promoting mlm scheme, and emails are difficult to pass by.

Anti-virus programs and major websites will warn you, if you just even try to visit an mlm program website, since there are lots of complaints against it.

I will also give you tip to marketing of mlm program at the end of this chapter

Below are some mlm marketers who have made it big

MATT LOYD

This guy has created his online mlm program, my online business empire, MOBE

I was unable to find his Facebook profile, these guys accounts get deleted since they try to promote mlm scheme, pyramid scheme, Facebook disallows mlm scheme advertising, they try various tricks and somehow manage to promote their products on Facebook, after few complaints there account might have got deleted

His Facebook link is
https://www.facebook.com/Learn-and-earn-internet-marketing-with-matt-loyd-701246539900579/

JOHN CHOW

This guy started from porn, then got into blogging,

John chow is a big name on internet, but he makes money by promoting pyramid scheme, MOBE
mlm marketing, I have seen him posting his revenue of over $100,000 on a single day, his per day income I have seen was easily over

$20,000 on any single day, just from a pyramid scheme MOBE alone, he also have other money making programs and they auto run, making him ton of money.

But don't follow this guy, he will only waste your time, by saying dream big, think big, he was so poor and how he made money by thinking, all unimportant crap information, which you already know. It won't help you even a bit.

I had purchased lot of his products, not even single was worthy enough, just lengthy videos and nothing good in it, his audio video courses were nothing but lengthy sheet filled stretched videos, if you watch his 5 hours video you will gain knowledge which if any useful is just of 1 minute or 2 minute, he just stretch his videos with unnecessary details and stretch, stretch and more stretch.

You must have watched network marketing videos, how they stretch there videos with so much unnecessary details, they show you there huge earnings keeps you glued and never tells you how they made it, they just fill their videos with unnecessary holy sheet, Like how can u make money by starting a blog, but in fact its total waste, you will waste your valuable time going through his videos, which tells you nothing, but to think big.

His products have more sale offers inside, once you buy his product, he will again recommend you to buy more programs, he lets you in cheaply, and then sells you lot of his other programs. He is shameless guy who keeps pestering you asking for more and more money, once you buy his 2nd product, he will recommend you his 3rd product. He has a chain of products which he recommends serially.

He is just not interested in seeing you succeed, he just wants your money, by spending time with him, and you won't get single cent valuable information, he will just show u how he is enjoying lavish life style by just starting a blog and joining a program, by seeing his lavish life style, you will want to follow him and you will buy his mlm program (pyramid scheme) and that's how he gets rich, that's how pyramid schemes work, by showing you the insane life style and motivating you to join there pyramid scheme

He will say the same thing again and again, using different sentences and words, all waste of time listening to his audio and video. He just brag about himself, how he makes money, how he enjoys life.

John chow services are like escort services who charges you just for being with them. ☺☺

You can check out his blog
http://www.johnchow.com/

Don't waste your time following him

ANKUR AGARWAL

This guy makes a lot of money from mlm marketing system, he is Indian "john chow", he joins almost all mlm programs and mint money from it, he is very successful in doing so, always on foreign tours, in a month almost 15-20 days he is outside India.

https://www.facebook.com/mlmquestionanswers?fref=ts

He started from Amway network marketing and since been doing mlm marketing,
he is just an expert in mlm thing

According to me, mlm is just circulation of money, there is no value in their products or services
you buy them just because you want to get into their program to make money, and there is also a legal risk into it. People who loose money complaints to the authority, how they lost money in a scam, and lot of complaints, force police to take action

"Speak Asia" was a survey pyramid scheme, it was regularly paying members, one news channel reporter made an issue, made a documentary about speak Asia fraudulent scheme, showed it on TV again and again, complained about it to the government, action was taken against speak Asia, all its main managers, managers, people on high post in that co. and also high commission earners were arrested.

The CEO of Speakasia stays in UK. Was saved from getting arrest, because Indian police cannot arrest someone who is not in India

Lot of top marketers of mlm products, I knew about, iam finding hard to find there profiles, may be Facebook deleted their profiles, these programs don't work for a long time

I think network marketing people are special breed, they get excited for nothing, speaking about making ton of money doing things absolutely of no value, they think deserve money because they think positive and think high.

MARKETING IN MLM

Marketing this online mlm product is hardest thing to do, since you cannot use traditional marketing methods, it is outlawed, and big advertising networks don't allow mlm advertising

You must understand the type of people who joins mlm programs, they are mostly house wives, old people looking for some employment, or very greedy people join it, or the people who wants easy money, without doing much, but its very tuff to market these products, new joines may sell it to his mom, relatives, and friends, but that's no way to market product

since you are selling it to people who are close to you, you will feel bad when they lose money, they just bought it, because you were selling it
there is no marketing technique if you are selling your product to your mom, dad, brothers, sisters, relatives and friends, I will explain how to sell it to people , real marketing

TRICK
The real trick is to sell people, who are looking for mlm programs to join or wants to make quick buck, you gona search these people, make them follow you, follow your blog and then you motivate them to join your system

Facebook and Google don't allow mlm advertisement, if they find it, they will suspend your account

But still few people manage and find ways to advertise on Google or Facebook

But when someone finds the trick, they complain, your ad will be immediately taken off, and your account might get disabled. Google bots also check violation of their AdWords ads.

You need to join mlm forums and its related website, there is data available of people who already are member of an mlm network, you can buy it, but it's very costly and data might be absolute and no 1 may convert, there are paid networks who claims they will promote your product for you and help you get more joinees, but it is way too costly and there is no guarantee that they will deliver joiners', you will lose money very quickly here

Most successful marketers do is, they promote themselves
show lavish life style videos and photos

Mlm marketers make videos explain their program, and gives out 1 or 2 useful tip and ask people to follow them or their blog for more information, they show their insane lavish life style, and attract people

Videos directly asking people to join there mlm program or any direct promotion of mlm product, might get your video deleted.
The trick is to give some good marketing tips in your YouTube video, ask them to follow you or join your blog, and then send him direct link privately in email

use upsell technique, the trick is make member pay at least $1 or $9 to get access to particular area of information, once the user pays, then you know that he has credit card and is ready to pay, then upsell higher value products to these users, this is what top mlm marketers do, before pitching their main product. Use words like $1 just to change your entire life style, people generally will try it.

Another trick is , it works on Facebook, always share good content on your page, all good quotes, amazing videos so people began to follow you, post photos of your lavish life style on your page, people will start asking you, what do you do, dude

I have seen lot of photoshoped pictures, a guy named 'soloman' photoshoped his image with the image of large house, claiming it to be his house, photo with BMW, photo with Audi Photoshop skills might help you in showing lavish lifestyle

Showing lavish life style is essential to motivate people to join under you.

EBOOK TRICK

This is the most commonly used technique to get followers, which even "john chow" and "Ankur Agarwal" use. Make a blog, have a mailing list for that blog. Give out a free eBook about "how to make money online", ask the visitors to join your mailing list for free eBook. You will have to use auto responder services like

http://www.aweber.com
http://www.getresponse.com
http://mailchimp.com/

Learn how to use these mailing services; this is how the most successful mlm marketers do it.

Once you join their mailing list, they send you emails motivating you to join their program.

SEMINARS
Organize seminars, I have seen this trick used by matt loyd to promote his program MOBE, they give Facebook ads for online seminars, which you can attend by paying a very basic fee, there ads appear "Learn how to be successful online" ,"Learn Internet Marketing" free seminar or paid seminar.

Giving such ads they make people join their blog

Facebook allows you to advertise to people who have liked specific page, or have specific interest.

There is lot of mlm marketers using Facebook to promote their mlm schemes

SHREWD OFFLINE MARKETING TECHNIQUES

The one technique which pisses me off is using your own friends to push sales to you. Like they hypnotize your friends who come to you pushing his mlm scheme and you are in a fix what to do about it, since you cannot say no to your friend.

I will explain how this unethical technique of marketing is used by M-way and Tupperware; these companies invest heavily in human psychology research and studies and find new ways to manipulate customers and forcing them to buy products which they don't need. It's like they are finding new ways to hypnotize humans in buying their products.

M-WAY TECHNIQUE
m-way trick, m-way is a shrewd beast being only company who survived so many years doing mlm, they ask their agents new joiner to give their friends product bags for free, tell them if there friends refuses to buy ask him to keep it for free and try it out. Once you keep his bag and try their products, you are obliged to pay now, since you feel guilty that you have used some ones product and not paid for it.

This is actually a well-researched technique, humans are evolved to return favors, give and take is inbuilt in human, even chimps have these tendency they keep track which chimp have gave them food, and which chimps how many times they have gave food.

Once you take favor you are automatically set to return it. It's an obligation.

TUPPERWARE PARTIES
Tupperware agents are asked to host parties and invite friends, and they host a party and invite friends, in the party mood is set such that all the attendees have to buy something all the party attendees buy something or they would seem like outcast. Since your friend is selling you have to buy it, and since everyone is buying you have to buy it. These companies are turning your close friends into zombies and turning them into their selling agents, party atmosphere is casual filled with your friends and acquaintances, and you cannot say no to your friends.

INSANE YOUTUBE EARNERS

Some people have figured out how they can mint money by making YouTube videos

FUNTOYZCOLLECTOR

CHANNEL IS
https://www.youtube.com/user/DisneyCollectorBR

This channel is not displaying name of the person who is running this channel or who the owner is, but this channel makes insane money, just by opening toys and playing with it. I never thought someone could make money by that.

They seem to be making over $5million every year. Quite a lot of money for just opening and playing with toys

Its pure luck, her videos are nothing but opening toys from plastic bags and playing with it, absolutely no production cost at all. She got nice fingernails though. Well to such kind of insane money, I can say she is directly blessed by "Allah" himself. For giving her such a idea and giving her so much money for almost doing nothing.

HULYAN MAYA

Their channel
https://www.youtube.com/user/iloveMayThing

This family has a YouTube channel which makes over one million dollars playing with toys, they make videos of a kid playing with toys and upload it on their channel. Great! Stuff

Super easy money, again absolutely zero production cost, and make money just by having fun

This family also seems to have received blessings from god.

ROSANNA PANSINO

HER CHANNEL
https://www.youtube.com/user/RosannaPansino

Her channel is mostly about desserts, cookies, cakes and chocolates, she has around 5 million followers, and she makes around $2.5 million per year doing it.

PEWDIEPIE

HIS CHANNEL

https://www.youtube.com/user/PewDiePie

This is an entertainment channel, which makes over $12 million every year, by showing entertainment videos on the internet.
he started his career by playing video games and uploading videos about video games, and that made him lot of money. No one even thought of that, playing video games can make so much money

He has a large following
https://www.facebook.com/PewDiePie

There is a production cost, but it is bear minimal and he also has acting skills.

ROMAN ATWOOD

HIS CHANNEL
https://www.youtube.com/user/RomanAtwood/featured

His channel is about pranks, he make videos doing prank and upload it on YouTube, he has over 8 million followers, he makes around $3 million annually.

LILLY SINGH

HER CHANNEL

https://www.youtube.com/user/IISuperwomanII

Her channel is about fun, she makes funny videos, she has good acting skills, her mimicry skills are also excellent. She has around 8 million followers, and makes around $3 million annually.

MICHELLE PHAN

Her channel

https://www.youtube.com/user/MichellePhan

Her channel is about makeup and beauty; she also was able to raise $100m in funding for her make-up delivery service Ipsy.

She has over 8 million followers, and makes over $3 million dollars annually just from YouTube videos.

KSI(Olatunji)

His channel

https://www.youtube.com/user/KSIOlajidebt

he started his channel, by uploading video clips of him playing and commenting on FIFA Video Games. Now he is into comedy, pranks and music videos.

He has around 12 million followers, and makes around $5 million annually just from YouTube videos.

RHETT & LINK

There channel
https://www.youtube.com/user/RhettandLink

These guys channel is about comedy, funny music.
their epic battle rap, "Nerd vs Geek", is the most popular video of theirs, below is its link, it had got over 28 million views.

https://www.youtube.com/watch?v=2Tvy_Pbe5 NA

They have around 4 million followers, and they make around $5 million dollars annually.

LINDSEY STIRLING

Her channel is
https://www.youtube.com/user/lindseystomp

Her channel is about playing violin music, and making videos doing it. Her music is good to listen and videos are also quite good. She has over 7.5 million followers and make around $6 million annually just from YouTube videos.

FINE BROTHERS ENTERTAINMENT

Their channel is
https://www.youtube.com/user/TheFineBros

These guys make funny video clips and upload them on YouTube, they have a very large following over 13.5 million followers, and they make around $9 million annually doing it.

JENNAMARBLES

Her channel

https://www.youtube.com/channel/UC9gFih9rw0zNCK3ZtoKQQyA

She is a 28 yr. old girl, with science degree, her videos are not about specific topics, but it's about her and she speaks about anything, but she has over 15 million followers, and she makes around $3million every year, just by being herself, and makes money uploading those videos, good girl.

She is more like Kim kadarshini of YouTube

A female who is good looking and can act crazy has a good chance here.

SKYDOESMINECRAFT

His channel

https://www.youtube.com/user/SkyDoesMinecraft

This Kid is about video games, he upload video games videos and makes around $2 -$3 million every year, has over eleven million subscribers
video game industry is bigger than movie industry, there is lot of money in video games

COLLEGEHUMOR

their channel

https://www.youtube.com/user/collegehumor

This is a YouTube channel with over ten million subscribers, its comedy YouTube channel, where two guys prank each other and make funny videos out of it

They make around $2-$3 million every year, but they do have to plan script and there is also a production cost for them

SECOND LIFE

Second life is awesome new way of social networking, in this world you can be anything you want, and connect with other people around the globe, it's a 3D social networking.

You can chat and even voice chat with other members, there are hotels, living room, beaches, dance pub, even prostitutes are available on second life, it's a video game with real people, people can talk, walk, fly change rooms, islands, hang around, can develop buildings, purchase and sell lands, create hotels, give rooms on rent, create avatars buy and sell them

I have heard that there are even terrorist's attacks in second life,

Second life has its own economy and currency, its currency is called Linden Dollars, L$

The exchange rate is constantly changing, but is generally between 270 to 300 Linden Dollars for 1 US Dollar.

Quite a few had made million dollars on second life and lot of people are making decent money, by creating avatars, selling lands, and developing hotels and giving them on rents

It's very interesting, people should try second life, and it is very addictive and interesting

Anshe Chung, the virtual land baroness, has apparently become the first millionaire in

Second Life. That's millionaire in real U.S. dollars. Her real-world persona, Ailin Graef, figures her net worth based on her substantial in-world land holdings, cash in "Linden dollars," which can be converted to real cash, as well as virtual shopping malls, store chains, and even virtual stock-market investments in Second Life businesses.

You can make money on second life by showing banner ads on your creation, selling avatars, creating hotels and renting or selling them out

Anshe Chung also appeared on"business week" magazine as the first second life millionaire

It's true you can make lot of money just by playing video games

You need to visit this website
http://secondlife.com/

Download and install the application

SURVEYS AND OTHER WAYS TO MAKE MONEY

there are online survey website, which pays to take their surveys, write reviews, there are numerous website available for that, do not pay to take surveys, they are fake.

The way the survey company works, they ask you to take a test survey to check whether you qualify or not for a particular survey, suppose survey is about Audi car, test survey will check whether you know about cars, whether you have a car, tried Audi car. By that way they understand that they are taking information from the right person

There are websites which pay you to write reviews about products, try this website

http://www.mouthshut.com

They pay good to write reviews, write comments, and so on

EVERYTHING TURNING INTO SOFTWARE NOW

Paper is the biggest pollutant, ranked 4th in terms of polluting industry, making paper is dirty, and it releases lot of harmful gases into air and harmful chemicals in water. Better the paper quality more the chemical used and more the pollution created

Paper making is dirty, Avoid paper and help the environment and also save trees.

Everything is getting digital, digital means everything connected; internet of things, Cisco Ceo predicts 40% of the companies of the whole world will be dead, only those companies will survive who turn into digital.

BOOKS

paper books will be replaced with digital eBook's, we can search in eBook's, copy paragraph, drill down, bookmark it, you can have 1000s of eBooks on computer or mobile phone, kindle is a good way to replace paper book, but problem with kindle that it's screen is too small, reading is somewhat painful, but wide variety of eBooks available on kindle and lot cheaper than physical books, and instantly available

South Korea has abandoned paper books, their elementary-level educational materials will be digitized, the entire school-age curriculum will be delivered on an array of computers, smart phones and tablets.

It is welcome move, since kids will have very less load to carry, and will save money on pen and paper

Reproducing eBook is easy, just copy and paste

MAGAZINES

paper magazines are already dead, although digital magazine subscription is available, with so much information already available for free; it's difficult for them to make money, too much information available and there is so little time. When videos and audios information is available who will take the pain of reading a magazine

NEWS PAPER

Newspaper is slowly dying industry, old people who are habitual to reading newspaper are still using it, but there are very few new joiners', and lot of old habitual people have given up reading news paper

People can download news App and read news on their mobile app or on computer; they can also watch news online.

DIGITAL CAMERA

Digital camera is dead now, why would anyone carry digital camera, when they can take pictures from their mobile phones

Kodak Company was shut down, its camera film business and digital camera was no longer required, since it was too slow to adapt to changes

135 year old company now dead

WATCHES ARE DEAD
wearing watches just to see time is extra burden now, since we can see time date, week on our mobile phone,
few people are using it, they are using it just for fashion, it is no longer necessary to wear watch for time, its sole purpose was taken away by mobile phone

I don't think wearable mobile watches will work, why anyone would have two things for the same work, he can just carry out his cell phone to see sms, alerts instead of seeing it in watch and then again carry out his cell phone to look in more details.

DESKTOP AND LAPTOP
desktop and laptop sales have taken a hit because of smart phones, but there are lot of things
can better be done from computers

Smart phones are very easy to use, even 2 yr. old kid can use it, by touch screen, using computers require little more skills, like typing, kid has to be at least 8 yr. old to use computer.

PAPER CURRENCY

Paper currency death is inevitable; it will just take few more years, that's where crypto currency roles comes into play, they are easy to carry it's just a number which you can carry in your mobile phone

Paper currency is no longer backed by gold, but by trust of the government who is printing it USA abolished gold standard, since there was not enough gold to back currency demand which was increasing, and gold prices were not in full control of the government, they were tied, so President Nixon finally abolished it.

BITCOIN

Bitcoin is a crypto currency which is widely used, it was almost $1200 in 2014, 1 Bit coin=$1200

it value felled because it got into legal trouble,

since it was widely used by silk road a drug selling website

Bitcoin can be tracked easily; purchase and sales trace can be tracked from start to end. So security is good, no 1 can steal bitcoin from you. If proper law and order is implemented

In future paper currency is bound to replace by some crypto currency for sure, at this time we are not sure which crypto currency.

Government currency may luse value, because they are printing currency at will, these paper currency are no longer backed by gold, they are in use because of trust

DOCTOR PRESCRIPTION

it seems doctors are very slow to adapt to new technology, they still use paper for prescription to patients

The current situation is that the doctor writes a prescription manually on the paper form. In addition to that, the doctor compiles a report indicating the number and type of prescriptions he has written. Patient brings the paper prescription to the pharmacy where the pharmacist enters the prescription into the pharmacy's information system, and then issues the medication.

Soon there will be digital prescription. This system will store the incoming prescriptions (messages), and based on a request it will issue the prescriptions of the specific patient to the information system of pharmacies.

The system enables to monitor and manage issuing of prescriptions.

The system will ensure an identical business-logic of medications and preferential prices.

The system will ensure an orderly circulation of treatment information.

The information will be very beneficial for health insurance.

Digital prescription will make sharing easy, so that doctors can better understand what's going on with the patient.

Digital prescription and results of the medication can be easily tracked; doctor can know what's working and what's not.

Its data can get into big data systems and algorithm can be made to see which medicines work the best for a particular type of disease.

DYING TV CHANNELS

There are only 24 hours for each and every individual, as more and more people are busy in social networks, YouTube, what Sapp, and websites, less and less time will be available for TV viewing and plus there are 100+ channels available, TV advertising doesn't work, since people switch to other channels whenever advertisement starts to show up.

Television Advertising is costly and it is difficult to track who viewed the advertisement.

Television industry is unable to develop any tool for who has seen the advertisement, no proper tracking for how many viewers have actually viewed the Ad.

Television can be watched on mobile phone and also on computer, but there is wide variety of content available on the internet, you can watch according to your preference

Internet TV is upcoming, whole internet will be available on TV, but still it's not good news for TV Channels, since lot of content will be available to the viewers, and their time is limited.

People don't like scheduled program any more, unless its sport event or any special event, most of the time they want instant gratification, which is available now with online web, where every TV show, every movie is available all the time.

MOBILE PHONE APP HYPE AND REALITY

Companies are pushing hard to develop their mobile app and install it to its users device, but truth is, it is not possible for user to install every available app, I myself installed Amazon and Flipkart app, but uninstalled it, since it disturbed me every now and then, by push notification, beeping my phone and showing new offer, ad every now and then, they must understand iam not in shopping mode 24 hours.

Pushing these ads irritates user, and the app gets uninstalled

So many messaging apps are available, and it is not possible to use all of them, I installed many of them, but uninstalled them, because of their irritating notifications, I just use whatSapp, companies are pushing hard to promote users their app, hike, Facebook messenger pushed TRAI to allow free internet basics, that is actually fake, Facebook just wants users to use only there application, they are trying to push for monopolistic trade practice.

Companies must understand just because I downloaded there application, iam not interested in every product they have, not everyone will install shopping apps, someone will do and almost 80% of them will uninstall, because of push notification, mobile beeps catches attention of the user, who might be busy in something else.

No one will install your mobile app, unless it is something unique or offer a very unique service, which no one else offers, people do not want to install app, unless it is very useful to them, because there is a securty risk in installing mobile app, and also it eats up space, and don't forget irritating push notifications.

Mobile apps are very attention grabbing, irritating, and distracting, so no working people or people who are busy with their life, would like to install another attention grabbing app and make their life miserable.

Mobile app opportunities are in internet of things, mobile phone communicates with other machine like car, TV your home

In future it is assumed that your mobile phone have more importance, it will do most of work, like reminding you to fill petrol, when petrol is low, car will tell your mobile that its low on fuel, and mobile will remind you of that

Most of the free mobile apps are in tracking business and selling their data to Axiom.

Importance of desktop computers and laptop will remain, since most of the people surf web for information, it is difficult to read on such a small screen of mobile device, people search for anti-aging methods, pills, lose weight, glow skin and that requires reading, lots of it.

There should be big opportunities in internet TV, since the screen Is big, features like video calling, conferencing will be breeze, internet TV is coming up, so be prepared for that, it will be virtually empty, and you could be one of the first few who can dominate it.

Samsung smart Tv are full Linux systems.

You can easily built Peer-to Peer skype like video calling and conferencing services for free, absolutely zero cost, by using WEBRTC technology.

Go search Google for Webrtc, if u is interested in making video calling services

Most free mobile apps make revenue by push notification, pushing ads to the users or getting there contacts and tracking details and selling it.

Push notification can be disabled both in android and IOS

I have noticed android have become spammy nowadays, even if we disable notification, it still popup ad notifications when we keep priority notification. This is dangerous for android, these spammy popups are highly irritating, seems to be popping every hour, I don't need discount on ola cabs.

If android continues to spam people, people will stop buying android phones.

WHAT TO BUILD

You need to have product which is good, if product is too good it can market itself

Build something, which is useful and society use it, like matrimony site, classified site and job site, yes matrimony, classified and job site, still works, but building a job site is very technical, and not recommended if you are in just for money, classified site will also require some extra work, But matrimony site is super easy to build and majority of people is interested in dating, you know porn was the biggest industry in early internet days, because sex was the thing, everyone was looking for, now people are there for socializing and information, porn is just too easy that people are not very much interested in it.

Porn is difficult to market, porn related stuff is difficult to host and its email is serious abuse, and lot of legal complications comes with it too.

My suggestions

1) Classified Site
2) Job site
3) Matrimony Site

CLASSIFIED SITE

classified site is very easy to build, and it is useful for the society too, since people use classified sites to buy and sell things, there are big companies just based on classified sites they are quikr.com, olx.in, craigslist.org.

Classified Sites are just easy to build and may not require staff at all to maintain, you may require few persons to verify listings, to avoid spam and adult postings, but that can be handled by algorithm, and may require just a single person to verify the postings, doubtful postings may be flagged and can be verified by human intervention

Classified site with Nosql(mongo dB) as backend, will still require some extra coding and extra work, since for each ad category will require some unique fields in the database, for example car table will have fields have automatic, semi-automatic, fuel type as fields, while mobile have fields like, touch screen, operating system, number of cameras, mega pixel of camera and so on

So listing ads of cars and mobile, will each have data fields different from each other, and there are several ad categories, like cars, trucks, pets, camera, services, jobs and so on, for each you will have to design specific page and that will increase your work.
It's easy, but not recommended.

We are giving free classified site source code built in asp.net mvc with mongo db as backend, we are using it ourselves, and you can download it at

http://www.codingpandit.com/

Job Site

Job site easy to build, and very useful for the society too, lot of people on the internet are searching for jobs, job site will require you some additional database skills, you will be storing each job seekers resume and will be providing employers search option, which will scan the resume and match the search criteria, it will put some heavy load on the computer resources, and will require you to do some tweaking.

You will need some additional skills to maintain database.

You can easily use our jobsite, which is built and tested with over 2 million members, we are using it.
It is built on asp.net mvc with mongodb as backend.

You can download it at
http://www.codingpandit.com/

Matrimony Dating Site

matrimony dating site, is easiest to build compared to the above two options, very few data fields and society needs it, everybody needs a life partner, it's easy to build and very easy to promote, because this niche covers bigger area, for example if you are website is about food, then your target area will be only food loving people, which are very few.

In this book, we will focus on building matrimonial dating site; I will explain design, sticky strategy and how to run it.

Matrimony/dating is big business, it is estimated to be over $2 billion worth industry.

Just by having website, won't make you rich, or else all the people with website would be rich, it takes design strategy, technology to make it work, you can easily compete with the big site, just because they have money that doesn't make them superior, technology and understanding users need will make you hit.

Big websites use "Big Data", so they can analyze customers, and figure out what they are looking for, and give them exactly what they want, so they come again and again for more

For example
http://www.buzzfeed.com/

Buzz feed, is just a blog , but its valuation is over $1.5 billion, it's because it analyses its user and show data which is relevant to that user, show jokes which is relevant to that particular user, it's difficult for a user to like and share your content, users only like and share content, by sharing, which makes them look good, intelligent to their friends and community, they will always share the quotes which support there notions, there ideas, which is of course difficult to guess, but buzz feed comes close to it, and see it's a big hit.

It uses survey to analyze user and his personality type

In matrimony site, you will have to analyze members like showing profiles which are relevant to him, like showing profiles to person of opposite sex, near to his location, with age gap preferences, religion preferences and so on.

TECHNOLOGIES TO USE

There are various technologies for web development, I will discuss some of them, and will recommend you the best in the end.

DATABASE TECHNOLOGY

MSSQL Server, MySQL, relational databases are not meant for high traffic website, for high traffic website, you will have to use NOSQL database, like Mongodb, Clusterpoint, Rethinkdb

Rethinkdb has a very good pub/sub feature, any changes will be pushed to the website immediately, it's cool feature, which is offered by firebase.com ,pubnub,

http://www.firebase.com
http://www.pubnub.com

If you use rethinkdb, you can have pub/sub feature for your webapp,

Mongodb is widely used nosql database it is very fast and easily scalable,

Clusterpoint has good full text search feature, if you are building a jobsite, you might think of using Clusterpoint
they are also offering free 10GB data storage, it will help you, since you won't have to manage database, you just have to use it.
https://www.clusterpoint.com/

Do some research on Mongodb, rethink db, Clusterpoint db because this is the databases you need to use for your mobile app and web app

Problem with relational database is its locking mechanism, when the record is accessed that record is locked and cannot be accessed by other queries, which queues up, and they are difficult to scale up, while Nosql database are very easy to scale

PhoneGap

No need to learn mobile programming language, you can simply code in html5, JavaScript and CSS and can build mobile phone apps

PhoneGap is a software development framework by Adobe System, which is used to develop mobile applications. To develop apps using PhoneGap, the developer does not require having knowledge of mobile programming language but only web-development languages like, HTML, CSS, and JavaScript. PhoneGap produces apps for all popular mobile OS platforms such as iOS, Android, BlackBerry, and Windows Mobile OS etc.

You can use Asp.net with WebDataAPi or node.js to provide data to your app using data url sharing

PhoneGap saves lot of time, since mobile programming languages are difficult to learn at first, and there are 3-4 popular mobile operating systems and you will have to learn 3-4 programming languages to learn to build App for every system

PhoneGap saves your time, and makes app building very easy

Web Technologies

iam explaining you some of the technologies, knowing many technologies will help you differentiate technologies its merits and its disadvantages

BOOTSTRAP AND MATERIALIZE

Bootstrap is the most popular HTML, CSS, and JavaScript framework for developing responsive, mobile-first web sites.

Bootstrap is a very good contribution to the web community, by Jacob Thornton and Mark

Otto, when they were working for twitter they invented it.

It's for web design; scripts will be loaded according to the device, assuming it is mobile first, accordingly scripts will be loaded.

Mobile phone have small screens, while tablet has a little bigger screen and computers and laptops have little more bigger screen. Bootstrap adjusts the design of the web page according to the screen size.

Before bootstrap, developers have to build two websites one for mobile phone and other for pc's.

Now with the bootstrap, developer just has to build one website, and it adjusts according to the user device and its screen.

Materialize is of the same purpose as bootstrap, but with one distinct advantage, responsive web design. When you click on the materialize object, it responds, making it very interactive and appealing, materialize designs are also very attractive.

Async/Sync.

You may hear many times in this book about async, traditional programming models were sync methods.

SYNCHRONOUS MESSAGING
Synchronous messaging involves a client that waits for the server to respond to a message. Messages are able to flow in both directions, to and from. Essentially it means that synchronous messaging is a two way communication.
In this method Sender sends a message to receiver and receiver receives this message and gives reply to the sender. Sender will not send another message until get reply from receiver.
One drawback of this method, sender will wait till he gets the reply from the receiver.

ASYNCHRONOUS MESSAGES
Asynchronous messaging involves a client that does not wait for a message from the server. An event is used to trigger a message from a server. So even if the client is down, the messaging will complete successfully.

Asynchronous Messaging means that, it is a one way communication and the flow of communication is one way only.
In this method sender doesn't wait for the receiver to reply, it moves ahead and carry another task

sync thread pools, eats up memory space of computers, so websites with high traffic shall not use sync methods, because they will eat up your cpu and memory space. That's why there is async, Async method has been added in almost all programming languages now, and even parallel computing is added in almost all programming languages, a basic computer now have at least 2 processors, parallel computing makes it easy to distribute work load to the processors. Now 2,3,4 computations can run parallel at the same time.

WEBRTC
Webrtc is a very disruptive technology, which you can use for making chatting system, video

calling system and games. Browsers in the past their role was, a clients who make request to webservers get the page needed and disconnect. Now with web 2.0 browser functionality has been increased.

Webrtc enables real time communications between browsers, without any plugins. Video chat applications built on Webrtc technology are much faster because they are peer to peer, no intermediary server required.

With just html5 and JavaScript knowledge, you can build Webrtc application.

There are many amazing applications built on Webrtc
like
https://www.sharefest.me/

It enables you to upload/download files peer to peer without using cloud.

Webrtc technology is heavily supported by Google; almost all browsers are Webrtc enabled.

Php/Mysql

it is the widest used technology for the web, its open source and lot of free source code is available for it
for example if you want to start matrimony site, you can easily find source code of full-fledged matrimonial website, you can find source code for classified site, source code for jobsite, basically lot of readymade free source code is available in Php/Mysql.

Drawbacks
Very slow, MySQL is also very slow if you hit high traffic, MySQL will crash, corrupt every now and then.

Although Php has evolved, updated and changed every now and then, and has been keeping up with the pace.
It has included parallel computing and async too, but still it is slow and takes lot of work.

Once your traffic grows, if you are using Php MySQL, you will have to rewrite the code, it's not recommended for high traffic website, I myself have used it and it is not good, database crashed every now and then, it could not cope with the IO

RUBY ON RAILS

Rails is a web application development framework written in the Ruby language. It is designed to make programming web applications easier by making assumptions about what every developer needs to get started. It allows you to write less code while accomplishing more than many other languages and frameworks.

Very few people use it now, very hard to find programmers, not at all recommended.

PYTHON/DJANGO

ok kind of technology, easy to understand code, python has lot of math functions, if your web app has lot of math's function, you can use this technology for your web app.

Google uses python for their search engine. Initially Google was using python only.

ASP.NET/MVC/ASP.NET 5

Microsoft is trying very hard to be the best, but it is far behind open source technology, they have added lot of features, but still it is cumbersome and very hard work

In asp.net mvc, if you add 1 column to your table you need to change the whole application, models and database design should match or else it throws and error, even if that column is not in use

You can make mobile app and website, using webapi for providing data, and html5 and angular for client side and then use phone gap to make android, ios and windows mobile app

Asp.net has an all-time support from Microsoft so finding solution for a problem would be easy, but still its lot of hard work to develop websites using it.

I have not seen any big websites using asp.net, asp.net also has forum, http://www.asp.net which provides you support, and they give answers to your questions and programming problems.

Asp.net 5 is open source; Microsoft is backing you if you are using asp.net, but still not recommended, it has a high learning curve, mvc framework adds lot of work without significant benefits.

METEOR.JS

Meteor is built upon nodejs technology, it's very fast to develop, coding is breeze and making web app and mobile app is lot easy, it uses JavaScript both on client side and server side, most of all its real time, whole website is single page app and its real time, such website will be difficult to do in asp.net or any other technology, but in meteor it is very easy and with few lines of code.

You can easily convert your web app into mobile app, it is built specifically for web,

Meteorjs has received 11 million dollars funding, and lot of work is going on, almost every day it's updated, more libraries and modules are added every now and then.

It has big community supporting it.

Problem with meteorjs, is that it requires intermediate level of Linux skills, hosting is pain, you got to know Linux very well, you cannot host it on windows

We have tried a matrimony site with 150,000 members on meteor, it was good but somewhat painful, and frequently app used to crash, and when the versions change it was very bad.

We are giving away our matrimony website built in metor for free; it has a good chatting system. It is available on our website http://www.codingpandit.com

SAILS.JS
Sailsjs is much like meteor built on node.js but it offers mvc pattern for web development, sailsjs has a big community but meteor has bigger community and it has received 11 million dollars funding, so I will recommend you can prefer meteor over sails.js

With very few lines of code you can add lot of functionality, it is built for the web and very fast

Node.js is actually very easy to learn if you are new to programming, if you are coming from asp.net, Php programming background, you tend to think in php, asp terms of programming, which is different and Node.js is altogether very different

Asp.net, Php uses threading model, while node.js is event based programming model, it's way too easy and requires very less coding, compared to Php or asp. Node is Very fast, and has a very less memory footprint

Always check the date of publication for tutorials and videos of nodejs, If you are following a tutorial and wonder why even when you typed the same exact syntax, your code doesn't work, Node is constantly evolving and almost updated every day, old code quickly becomes absolute, and because it is getting updated so frequently and new features are getting added rapidly, the tutorials you are referring are most likely to be old, the code was working then, now it's not working, because the module versions its referring have been updated and it no longer works, if you are writing the same code, the code and tutorial is absolute now, and its code will not work.

I will recommend you use node.js for your web app, it's not that difficult as it looks, use KOA framework for your node app, instead of express

Node with koa framework with mongodb+Angular or Reactjs

Node with express framework is difficult to code and difficult to read because of so many callbacks, and error handling is also difficult, it will be soon be replaced by KOA, so use only the latest technology since node is very frequently updating, your code with express may not run in the future

Although meteor is very easy to code, and it has received 11 million dollars funding and has a big community to support it, but Problem with meteor you will have to use Linux for your webserver, Installing meteor app on that Linux server will require you to have Linux technical skills, nginx skills and docker skills, it's way too complicated even for well to-do Linux user, same is true for sails.js

While app built directly on node can be installed on windows on iis, and request for a particular website can be forwarded to node server, so administration is quiet easy.

Node.js is used by big websites and big companies
linkedin.com is built on node
Wal-Mart is using it
yahoo, Google and Microsoft are also using it.

If you are JavaScript expert Nodejs is recommended

ANGULAR JS
Angularjs is a JavaScript framework which helps you make single page web apps.

You can learn more about it
https://angularjs.org/

It also has simple video tutorials to make you understand.

Angularjs is developed & supported by Google and has a huge community.

REACTJS

Reactjs is JavaScript framework built and managed by Facebook.

It doesn't directly work on the dom, but on the html string making it much faster.

It claims to be faster than angular and easy to learn, Angularjs doesn't have linear learning curve, you will learn fast in the initial stages and then you will get stuck.

It is estimated that Angularjs is going to do some major changes, which will make you relearn it.

SCRUM METHODOLOGY

Traditional method was plan everything ahead and then start doing it this method is called "Water Fall method", but its absolute now, because no 1 is exactly sure what he needs.

use SCRUM methodology; it is basically build features which are in immediate need and launch the application as soon as you can, by launching the application you get feedback you need, so that you can go back and refine your application.

Basically nobody has complete idea, about what actually he needs; it's just a cloudy idea, lot of things which started to be something and end up being something else

For example ms-word has over 1000 features, but nobody uses them, users are not even aware of all the features available in ms-word. So basically developers focused on developing features which no 1 will use, thus wasting valuable resources on it.

Scrum way will be build the application with the most useful features and launch the application and then with the users feedbacks and suggestions add more features accordingly, by this way we avoid wasting time on features which nobody needs.

Scrum methodology is used in almost all software companies now.

Scrum helps you build fast, test your idea, if it fails, you fail fast and save your time and resources

WEB HOSTING TO USE

You need to have good web hosting for smooth functioning, I have used few of them and reviewing them, but companies adapt and change from time to time

Hosting is a technical part, so best handled by hosting company and their technician; when you buy the hosting make sure technical burden of hosting is taken by the web host, not by you

Hosting must come preconfigured with all the software's necessary

For the purpose of safety, I will advise you to use different companies for both domain name registration and hosting services

For example, if you use godaddy.com for registering your domain, do not use it for web hosting, use different web hosting provider for ex server intellect.

If there is spam and abuse complaints, and if you are hosting it with the registrar, registrar might suspend your domain, disable your hosting but if your domain is registered with godaddy and you are using "server intellect" for hosting, then if any complaint goes to godaddy.com they cannot suspend your hosting, because your hosting is on different servers, if server intellect gets complaint about you, they cannot suspend your domain, they can suspend your hosting, but your domain is safe you can at least redirect your domain traffic to other website

Most abuse and spam complaint will be made to your hosting company, so your domain will be safe most of the time

GODADDY.COM

it is the number one in hosting services, domain registration is easy and with lot of options available in the domain and hosting control panel, management is ease.

Godaddy.com is very strict on abuse and spam complaint, I myself had problems with them, in the past with just one complaint, your domain will get suspended, and their abuse department don't work on weekdays, you will receive some automated emails and you have to agree to all conditions, then they will ask you to pay a fine for wasting their time, again you will have to agree on all the conditions they mention, your domain will remain suspended until you agree on all the conditions they mention

Once my domain got suspended for a very small reason, and they did not hear my side of the story, I got an email and was asked to agree on all the conditions, I replied with my side of story, which they don't even look at it, they had some algorithms which check contents of the email, if you agree all of them, then only it is seen by human, until then your domain remains suspended, I agreed all the conditions and also paid a fine. I hardly had any choice

Now godaddy.com emails you first asking for justification, if you fail to prove them, they ask you to pay a fine or else they suspend your domain

Use godaddy for domain registration, keep it dormant for 2 months, after that host it on another service, like everdata.com or serverintellect, if someone make abuse complaint to godaddy, you can move the domain easily, but you got to stay atleast 2 months with the registrar after that you can move your domain

BLUEHOST.COM

I also tried bluehost.com, there servers are not very good, even simple WordPress blog was not working well on their servers, wordpress.com recommended me to use bluehost, as it was first on their preferred list, and I tried it.

SERVERINTELLET.COM

I used their services for around 2 years and it's good, I never had any problems with them, their support was excellent, but there services are bit pricey.

POWERVPS.COM

its good, cool, support is excellent, I had used their services for around 3 years, absolutely no problem with them

EVERDATA.COM

Extremely good, no problems at all, I had used them for over 2 years, and they are good, support is excellent and they go extra mile to help you.

SOFTSYSHOSTING.COM

extremely poor support, paid support is very costly, and they offer no money back.

In the past i had purchased vps from them for web hosting, but they did not install control panel and mailing software with it, It was just vps with windows server, it didn't have mail server and control panel installed, I told them they didn't have all the software's needed to start a website, they said I can install them, but they don't provide support to third party software's.

Iam a web guy not a server admin, if I install them and if it doesn't work according to the expectation, who is going to fix it.

In my case server was not preconfigured with all the necessary software's to start a website, they were asking me to install them, which is quite technical and no guarantee it will work.

Now I once again visited there website, now there servers come preconfigured with email software and control panel

When I purchased that time it was not available, I posted about them on forums so that others know,

You can see the issue I had
http://www.webhostingtalk.com/showthread.php?t=699328

I posted about them on the webmasters forum and their arrogant replies.

When you buy a server for web hosting, it shall come with all the software's needed to start a website, we cannot research and install all the software needed, one can get very busy in fixing the issues rather than starting a website.

I recommend VPS or Dedicated Server for the matrimony website, since the web software's source code iam giving out which you can use, won't work on shared hosting.

I will recommend everdata.com or server intellect

WHAT TO BUILD AND MARKET IT
you can build anything you want, but for the example sake I will be using dating/matrimonial site, because it is easy to

build, easy to market, everybody needs someone,

Everybody is so busy in there career, almost all of them are getting late for marriage, they simply don't have time for love, so plenty of singles out there

Matrimony dating website has huge income, plentyoffish.com (pof.com) makes over $20,000 per day. Just by showing Google ads. Search about plenty of fish ad revenue on YouTube and Google.

You can also check "Tinder" mobile dating app, a huge hit

You can also charge subscription fees, but getting merchant account has been difficult recently lots of rules and regulations.

You can also start gay, lesbians website with the same website code, code is freely available on

http://www.codingpandit.com/codes/viewcode?codeid=5698c57b215545106c3d0c1d

It's fully functional meteor source code, written by me; you can download it free and use it, source code is used with over 1.50 lac members, and it was fine with no problems, it also has chatting system, location based matches and so on.

Although iam giving you "dating" website source code
made in meteor, you can use it as a test, or you can find some programmer to tweak it according to your needs, and host it, that source code has all the necessary features for starting a dating website.
You can download it and immediately start dating website, in the mean time you can develop your dating app in node and angular, later you can replace that meteor dating app, with app built in node.

Meteor app hosting needs Linux skills; you will need to have atleast vps, with Ubuntu as operating system, with nginx and docker installed.

Even if you use cloud services, which claim to do meteor hosting, they say are easy to use, but they also requires intermediate level Linux skills. I suggest you to use vps, because vps will be cheap, if your website receives good traffic, cloud will be costly.

This meteor source code won't work on shared hosting, so far till this date there is no shared hosting for meteor apps.

WEB SITE DESIGN STRATEGY

Build website with Html5 and angular for client side, and use asp.net webDataApi or node.js to provide data sharing via url
with html5+ angularjs, you can easily build mobile app, by using phone gap, just make your app in JavaScript and html5 and phone gap will convert your app into android app, iPhone app and windows app.

See the advantage here, you don't have to create separate app for android, iPhone, and windows, so this has saved your lot of learning time, just JavaScript and html and you are able to build mobile app.

USE G+ FOR WEBSITE REGISTRATION

Simple. Easy. Fast = More sign-ups! Permission-based contact details like email ID can be pulled in from the social networks. Most people only have one social profile on each network, making the retrievable data more authentic. Fake emails will no longer penetrate your sign-ups!

Google will also know that its user is using your app, so whenever he does search which might be relevant to your website, your website link will be more relevant for him and it will appear in his search result, Google knows your website is important for them since he has signed up to your website

I will not recommend using Facebook for signups, since when I was using it, it changed its options frequently and added deleted features so frequently that Facebook signups were simply not working, constantly I had to change the code, and its api was difficult to understand.

I myself had problems coding with Facebook Api, my programmers had hard time coding with Facebook api, we had to outsource our Facebook api coding to other software company.

MAKE USERS FEEL AT HOME
When users signup and allow you there contact detail, check out their friends with email ids in your database, if some of his contacts are already signed up, then you can show their profiles to him, that way the user will feel more comfortable, since he is not alone, his friends are also using your website, he will feel good when he finds the people who he knows, are also using your website.

SHOW MEMBERS WHAT IS RELEVANT TO THEM
Why Facebook shows more and more content you like, it's because they don't want to piss you off,
showing content which is irrelevant to the user will irritate him, and make him un-register, delete his account.

In case of your matrimony website, showing opposite sex profiles which is near to his location will be very relevant for the user, that's why Tinder Dating App is hit.

DISALLOW DELETE

Every website has option for user to remove his profile from the website, you shall also have that option, but instead of direct delete, use "Delete request" option, asking the user why he wants to delete his profile, ask him the reason, the reasons they give will help you get valuable feedback of your website, you shall be able to see delete requests in your admin panel, don't delete it immediately give some time, user may remain, if he requests again, then delete his profile.

Large number of users is necessary to attract large number of registration.

HAVE CHATTING SYSTEM

Chatting system helps people stay on your website for longer time. Chatting is addictive, if you have chatting system on your website; you will find that many people will come again and again just for chatting.

GETTING TRAFFIC

Getting traffic techniques will differ from country to country, in India for matrimony dating website males outnumber females, so getting females on the website will be priority, take efforts to make beautiful females register on your website, pay them if you can, because those females gone attract more registration, I myself paid beautiful females to register on my website and to chat, phone chat, video chat with other members, it works

There are also nude chatting websites and have high traffic
http://www.omegle.com/

This website is very high valued and have lot of traffic, one of my friend frequently chats on it, he says he always find girls who nude chat with him

I think this website pays to female members to nude chat with members.

JUST STARTED HOW TO PROMOTE
What to do if you newly started website, absolutely don't have any mailing list. And have no members or very few members.

If you have very few members, don't show any members or members count on your front page, restrict page access to members only, have your front main page designed beautifully and give option to register without revealing much detail.

Best thing to promote your website will be to use Google AdWords coupon, Google gives free credit for new advertisers, in India it gives around Rs 2000/- free credit, in some countries Google gives $100 free credit for advertising. You can use this credit for free advertising, ask your friends, relatives to register on AdWords, use their advertising credit to promote your website.

Lot of websites offer free credit, coupons for AdWords, godaddy.com offers AdWords coupons and credit for its customer.

Iam sure Facebook also must be offering free advertising credit for new advertiser, look out for that.

Use any free credit offered to you by any advertising network.

I myself have used free advertising credit from Google, Microsoft and yahoo.

USING SOCIAL MEDIA

Use Google+ and Facebook and get some traffic from it too.

Register a hot girl fake profile on both these social networks, tons of friend requests will follow; you can share your website url in your social network, this trick works.

Be aware of Facebook, they will ban you, if you have too many friends in very short time, even Google+ is problematic but not as problematic as Facebook

I was surprised to see that Google+ communities bring lot of traffic, share relevant url with good looking girls pics in appropriate g+ communities

Share just 1 in high traffic communities posting the same url 2 or 3 g+ communities, might get you ban,

Posting the same post in lot of different community might get your G+ account disabled. If you do the same post in more than 2 G+ community, it will most likely be marked as spam and users won't see it, you will be able to see it, since you posted it, but no other members would be able to see it.

G+ has algorithm for spam posting, it also sometimes mark spam legitimate post as spam.

I have noticed both Facebook and Google+ gives low visibility to the posts which has website url in it.

EMAIL MARKETING
Email marketing works, it is still very effective, even with some spam complaint problem, I will tell you one simple technique which works best, without any spam complaints

Write an email, without any url, if you input url then it will be spam and the receiver can complaint,
when the user complains, you will have to prove that it was not spam, show them the ip

address from where you got the email, and so on, if godaddy.com is hosting your domain, you are in big trouble, they used to suspend the domain immediately, now you have to prove that it's not spam, pay a fine and they make you agree on lot of things, now they ask for proof to prove that's it's not spam, and if you can't prove they will charge a good fee for wasting their time.

There are lots of spam trap email ids, which may get into your mailing list, once you mail to those emails, it will be immediately reported as spam, and you will be in trouble, they are actually unnecessary harassment, so your first priority will be to remove those spam trap email ids.

Purpose of some companies is to report spam, they get rewarded for it, there are millions of spam trap email ids which are circulated on the web, posted on website, so when someone harvest email ids, he also harvest spam trap email ids. And emailing to these spam trap email ids will get you into trouble, they will immediately report it to your hosting company, and hosting company might suspend your hosting account.

Spam trap companies had shut down many websites in the past.

How will you remove those spam trap email ids?, spam trap email ids are difficult to filter out, there are some companies which manually filter out your mailing list for spam trap email ids for you, for a fee, but still it's not full proof, so email only to those public email providers like, gmail.com, yahoo.com, Hotmail.com, rediffmail.com to avoid spam trap email ids.

You can remove all AOL.com and Hotmail.com email ids, because they make lot of complaints, I myself have deleted all aol.com and Hotmail.com email ids, they create lot of spam complaints, even for genuine emails they complain spam, AOL is worst in case of spam complaints.

I have seen AOL actively, purposely mailing into auto responders and then complaining about spam, I have received spam complaints from aol, even though I don't have any AOL email ids in my database.

To reduce spam complaints, you can email without url, for example if you are running a matrimonial website?, you can write

"Are you interested in marriage?", you can see there is no website url in this email content, send it as first email, then have an auto responder set, so when the user replies you can auto email your website link for him to signup

Emails with subject "Hiya", works best, they are most likely to be seen and opened.

Auto responder example

1st email, with subject "hiya" and email content "are you interested in marriage?"

2nd email when the receiver of email, replies to your email, then you can send second auto responder email with url to your website

2nd email example below

That's glad you are planning to get married, we have lot of profiles which can suit you please create a profile on our website http://www.yourwebsite.com,

So that we can help

Now you can see, in the first email, there is no website url, so the receiver cannot complain, lot of hosting companies require website url to say it's a spam, no website url, no spam.

Even if the user complains, you can always say it doesn't have any url, and nothing happens,
and if the user complains as abuse for second auto email, you can give proof, that user has emailed you, there is prior contact and that's not spam or abuse, complain will fail.

If your website is very new, it will be difficult for you to pass Gmail, yahoo, Hotmail you will have to change the email content frequently

When Google notices millions of users have the same email, they know its spam

Be wary of bounces, if you have too many bounces, all your emails will be blocked for few minutes, hours, days, it depends on the email receiving server rules, and it will cause a huge spool on your server consuming your memory and sometimes crashing your server. Don't email to users who don't want your emails, because they will mark your email as spam. Google, yahoo uses user's feedback for spam detection.

Always use working email id to send emails, check your emails, check complaints, check bounces, solve complaints and remove bounces

Working email id means for example if you send email by the name peter@yourwebsite.com, peter@yourwebsite.com must be actual email address, where it can also receive emails, email id which cannot receive emails back are most likely to be marked as spam.

Email marketing has become very technical today; you will need to have technical skills to manage mailing from your server. There is IDS system, Abuse, Spam detection systems, built right into your server system. Mass mailing is easily trapped and emails are blocked from getting sent out, even "smartermail" email software has IDS, abuse, spam detection system, it will block your own ip, if you mass email; it has spam prevention libraries built into it. You will have to check logs, and see if emails are actually getting delivered.

That's why I tell you need to have technical skills to be able to run a large website.

Every day Google, yahoo adds new rules for spam detection, so you need to stay updated for this.

REVIEWS
Google loves reviews and comments, that's why they tried to purchase yelp.com for ½ billion dollars but later purchased Zagat Reviews are important to Google, since it

wants to display the best search results, best things to the searcher, it can analyses comments and review and can determine if its positive or negative review

Try to get as much reviews about your product on these product review sites, this can help your search engine ranking.

When lot of people comment on a particular info page, Google knows that something important is going on that page, and it scores a higher preference in search result

Over the years Google has become very sophisticated; its machine learning can analyze words and understand them.

GOOGLE SEARCH – ORGANIC MARKETING METHOD
In Web 3.0 now its relevancy
Google search has changed now, it uses social connection to show you result, suppose if your friend is using a particular website, and you are in his friends list, if you are searching for something related to that website, which your friend has link or is following it, then it will

show that website which your friend is using, because Google thinks if your friend is using it, then it is more relevant to you.

Have your website link in your Google+ and Facebook profile, have something on your profile, that lots of people add you, follow you.

Now when they search or their friends search, your website link will be preferred for them, since they follow you or have you as friend or there friend is your friend or follower, your website becomes more relevant to them

HAVE AN AFFILIATE PROGRAM

have an affiliate program on your website, it shall available to all the members who join your website, give them incentive to promote your website, give them ready made message to paste it into their email and send it to friends, this thing works, because friends invite there friends, there is no spam and it works better

Give them text links, with their affiliate id; give them banners code so they can paste it on their website. In short make them your website promotion easy, by giving the required tools and tutorials.

Give them tips about how to do promotion, ask them to post their affiliate link on their Facebook, Google+ page, ask them to do classified ad posting with their affiliate links. This will also help you in search engine ranking.

Adding an affiliate program to your website is easy, even a basic level programmer can do it.

Keep affiliates cookie just for 1 day, or some 1 might do cookie seeding like Shawn Hogan and fraud you.

MAKE VIDEOS

Making videos and uploading them on YouTube, Videos can also be used to promote your website or product, it might not suit for promotion of matrimony website, videos are best suited to promote health care products, mlm programs.

DRAFTING NEWS

Ever heard a story wife selling her husband on ebay?, how they find lost friend on a particular website, found lost mom on particular website.

These are stories created to market the website, lots of these stories are fake, they are created to capture your attention and make you aware of their website.

Newspaper, television channels are paid to publish this news, actually it's not a news, but advertisement.

You too can use such technique to market your website, make people aware of your website, by publishing an exciting and emotional story.

Politicians also make very good use of this technique, they pay news channel to publish about them. They pay to highlight their work, how they stood against some righteous issue,

how they fought for you, how that politician made into politics by hard work and dedication and social service, they highlight his achievements
and bring positive attention to him.

Movie maker pays news channel to promote controversy related to their movie or any of the movie actors, which then brings attention to the movie.

A simple statement of actress is shown again and again on TV, as if some nuclear bomb has fallen, actually they are paid to do this.

I have seen one Indian model (calendar girl of kingfisher) "poonam pandey" news publish every now and then on yahoo and on news channel.

Her activities were like, she will get naked if India wins the world cup, and she will get naked if "Narendra Modi" becomes prime minister.

It was like she will get naked for anything. She just needed a reason to be naked.

This is a cheap technique to bring attention to ourselves, create controversy and then land up job in movies, TV serial and big boss.

Yahoo used to publish articles about her, even though she is not a big star. I think she paid yahoo to promote herself, even her yoga session, her trips to hotels, her earnings all were in the yahoo news.

This trick worked, she got the attention she needed, lot of Google search were made for her, when she announced she will get naked if India wins the cricket world cup, she also received more Facebook followers, it works.

You see why upcoming actress and models have affairs with famous sports star, by having affairs with sports star, they make into news, which bring them attention and get them job in big boss or some movies.

Indian actress "dipika padukone" made it successfully into movies by having relationship with cricketer "yuvraj singh", she got famous doing it. She was in the everyday news, her price tag increased for a movie, because of her popularity and controversy she created.

Actually it's a publicity stunt, to get attention.

Talent is the main factor but getting attention is also another factor to be successful in movie industry. That's why so many talented rappers are still not famous in spite of being very talented, they simply lack the technique to get attention, and they failed to create any controversy for attention.

Even pharmacy companies are also spreading crafted hyped news.
For example a news story that a person lost his finger in an accident but fortunately his brother was working in some pharmacy company, and he had some revolutionary technology in his company, pig bladder powder, which he applied on his finger for months and then his finger grew back. This is a "made up news", I have seen this news on many websites, nobody verified it, they just published the journals released by this pharmacy companies. If it was true, then why it happened only once, only with that particular

old man whose brother was working in pharmacy company, Why not again n again.

Pharmacy Company does this to bring attention to them, so that they get new investors, investments. Their products get more sales in the market, because they always have some revolutionary technologies.

News channel is mostly paid media; I almost got into printing newspaper business, I was told that local newspaper make money by not publishing the news, it's by coercing the illegal business or wrong doing, collecting money from them to keep quiet, not printing about them.
Print ads revenue is so low that it cannot even cover news printing cost.

Attention is very costly, we all are very busy and can only pay attention to one thing at a time. So we filter out which is not important and pay attention to only things that matter or something which is abnormal or out of the way of our normal understanding. Getting attention is a science and you will find lot of tutorials for it, search Google.

News channel are always looking for exciting content to grab attention of its viewers, increase their viewership or print circulation, they always wants some kind of breaking news, even if they know it's doubtful they will still publish it with just little proof to support it.

ONLINE ADVERTISING

You can also advertise online on Google and Facebook, I will explain more about it, there are many online networks other than this two, but since Google and Facebook they are the biggest ad networks, I will cover them

FACEBOOK ADVERTISING

Facebook advertising or social media advertising has some distinct advantages over other media of advertising like television, radio

Users can engage with your product, with you or your brand, there is two way communications

Facebook allows you to advertise to its members, you can advertise based on the page he likes, his age, his country, and can filter your advertisement to your exact audience.

This sounds great, since you can target exactly the kind of people you are looking for.

It depends on the purpose of your advertising, if you are looking for more registration on your website, or more likes to your page, branding and so on

I myself tried Facebook advertising and my goal was to get more signups to my website

I failed to get signups to my website, wasted lot of money

Facebook advertising is waste of money, as per my experience in relation to get more signups, I have spent at least $1200 experimenting on Facebook, and I was unable to make it work

I will also tell you the reason, once you setup your ad targeting your audience,

The people, who already liked your page, see your ad, he is supposed to see it anyway, but you are charged for that

The people who already clicked on your ad, is shown your ad again and again, that's waste, that person has already clicked on your ad and might have already signed up to with your website, showing him your ad is waste, you are also charged for that.

People just like your post or comment, and do nothing, they don't sign up to your website, click on that ad, just like it without even seeing it, that's a waste of your money.

Facebook is reluctant to send visitors to your website; it is designed to keep people glued on their website

Facebook is not good for advertising, if you want more registration on your website, Facebook simply doesn't want their users to leave their website

Facebook has some advantages for particular type of marketing, for example political campaign, one can create a political campaign

or create a page, to reach his voters
that can encourage supporters to like your
page and spread your political cause, raise
funds

American President "Obama" party made good
use of Facebook advertising to win elections.

In India, Prime Minister "modi" BJP party, also
made good use of Facebook to spread their
messages, they made funny mocking videos of
opposition parties and they were spread like
wild fire by people.

BJP party was more tech savvy, while its main
rival party congress were very slow to adapt to
digital media, they continued with their old
ways of advertising, using TV ads and print
media

BJP was the first to adapt sms campaign; they
were mass sending political messages sms to
the people

Modi supporters liked his page, and his
messages were shared among their friends.

Modi Team came up with catchy and innovative slogans, which were spread like wild fire

Advertising Gurus like Sam Balsara, Piyush Pandey and Prasoon Joshi were the ones who created catchy slogans like "Janta Maaf Nahi Karege", "Ache Din Anne Wale hai".

These catchphrases became viral on social media as well. And "Ab ki Baar Modi Sarkar"had become a tag line of BJP as well.

Advantages of social media advertising over TV and Radio Advertising is that user can engage with you or your product, there is two way communication, but in case of TV, Radio its one way message

In our case, we are looking for more registration on our website, Facebook advertising is not recommended

Facebook does not allow dating and matrimonial website ads anyway.

GOOGLE ADWORDS ADVERTISING

AdWords is Google's paid advertising product. Have you ever seen those ads that appear at the top or side of your screen? Those are AdWords ads that a company paid for so that people will notice their business

AdWords ads are also shown on millions of websites of AdSense publishers

Whenever a user is searching using certain keywords, you can trigger your ads to these keywords,

For ex. If you are website is dating site, you can set ads to certain keywords, like bride, grooms, dating, life partner, whenever someone types these words in Google search, your ad will be shown to them.

This kind of advertising is much targeted, since these ads are shown at the right moment, the moment he is looking for that product or information.

If you want more signups to your dating website, you can use AdWords to advertise just on their search engine and not on AdSense network.

A person searching using Google is most likely looking for more information about the particular service or product and most likely to take action.

If you are using keywords like "dating", "friend finder", "soul mate", "friendship"

If you are promoting your dating site in AdWords, if a person comes to your website, via Google search typing your ad keywords like "dating"," soul mate", "friendship" is most likely to register, since he was looking for dating site, soul mates, friendship

While in case of AdSense network, user just happens to visit your website, it's not very targeted

There is a trick in getting your AdWords ad more visibility in Google search

Your ad must contain keywords the searcher is typing.

For example

If the user has typed "dating" in Google search

For Your ad to appear more, use dating keyword in your ad like this

Your AdWords ad should look like this

Dating in India
Find dating partners in
your area
http://www.yourwebsite.com

You see this ad has keywords dating; dating keyword appears twice in this advertisement. So it is more relevant and will be shown more often. It is also more likely to get clicked, increasing the relevancy of your ad, and your ad will be shown even more, Google also use ad performance metric in showing ads, more the ads are getting clicked for particular keywords, more the ad will appear for those keywords.

Google also checks your website for the ad relevancy, it also suggests keywords to you based on your website, if your website is about dating, it will more likely to appear for the dating keyword.

I have also seen page rank gets increased, when you do AdWords ad, goggles logic, if you are spending money to advertise your business that means you are very serious about it.

Create as many ads as you can for particular campaigns, using the search keywords in your ad.

Your ad will appear often, you will be able to generate good converting traffic to your website via AdWords.

I was successful in getting lot of registration from AdWords, with per click cost as low as 0.80 paisa.

If you allow your ad to appear on Google AdSense network, you will get lot of traffic, but that won't convert much, since the people who will be visiting your website, just happens to visit your website, with no real intention of registering on your website.

AMAZON MONEY

Amazon affiliate program is a great way to make extra income, when someone clicks on your affiliate link and visit amazon.com, that click is valid for 24 hours, like when someone visits amazon.com clicking your affiliate link a cookie will be created by amazon.com on his computer and later when he makes the purchase within 24 hours, you will be credited with the sale.

All you need to do is to drive people on amazon.com by clicking your affiliate link

Here is the simple way, you can do it

Create a website, which offers free kindle eBooks, some authors offer their eBook for free for few days to get reviews

Check out this website

http://www.enlightenme.education/

The whole objective of the above website is to drive traffic to amazon, kindle eBook readers are mostly people who have purchased kindle eBook reader, that means they have credit card and are frequent buyers of eBooks, when some goes to amazon by clicking on your affiliate link, a cookie will be created on his computer and then later any time within 24 hours, the user comes back to amazon.com and make purchase any other thing, you will be credited for sale and you get nice commission for it.

You can join affiliate program here

https://affiliate-program.amazon.com/ (for America Residents)

https://affiliate-program.amazon.in/

(For people from India)

You need to check where the customer is from to send him to appropriate amazon website

Suppose if customer is from United states, and you send him to amazon.in website using your affiliate id from amazon affiliate program from India, you won't get credit for sale, since at the time of purchase that person will be redirected to amazon.com where you won't be registered as an affiliate, so register for affiliate program for each country, like

Register for amazon.uk, amazon Australia, amazon India, amazon Canada and so on

Send customer to appropriate amazon website, depending on the location of amazon customer.

I mean to say send customer from America to amazon.com, send customer from Britain to amazon.uk, send customer from India to amazon.in

If you don't understand what iam saying, just read again

AMAZON REVIEW VIDEOS

This is the most easiest and honest way to make good money from the internet.

When the user has decided to purchase a certain product, he is looking for reviews to make a final decision

For example, if someone decides to purchase iPhone 6s, he will search Google for its reviews, he will visit YouTube to know about its features and use from customer who have actually bought and used that product.

There are whole lots of individuals who are making a living making review videos or reviewing products

Check out this guy's video

https://www.youtube.com/watch?v=_eewlRCfewQ

He is reviewing "amazon echo", check out his views, and check the below of this video, you will see his affiliate link towards amazon

He is getting paid 2 ways, he is getting paid by YouTube by showing ads on his video plus he is getting paid by amazon for bringing sales.

You can easily make lot of money reviewing products and that's easy stuff anyone can do

PLAYING VIDEO GAME AND MAKING TON OF MONEY

Idea of hard work, dedication, long term commitment sounds bull sheet, when you can see people making money playing and enjoying.

This is the stuff you will actually laugh and will say, god why didn't I knew it first.

There are few people who have become millionaires, just by playing video game and uploading a recording of it on YouTube

There is lot of money in video games; there are sports competitions of video games, international competition of video games and the prize money is usually million dollars

Even though there is lot of money in video games, it's not for me, iam a mature man and has a life, if you love video games and you spend plenty of time in it, then you can easily make money just by recording your video game clip and uploading it on YouTube

Check out this video

https://www.youtube.com/watch?v=3KJs9ZVK ZEo&feature=youtu.be

You see the above video is just recording of that guy playing video game, he has almost done nothing, he just played the video game and recorded it via screen recorder

Look at the subscribers of this guy, and look at the views he got for his video, he is definitely making 1000s of dollars.

To use this technique all you got to do, is download the video game and install it and download "Camtasia Screen Recorder" or you can download Fraps

I will recommend fraps, http://www.fraps.com/

I have used it myself and its cool.

If you do not have any idea of video games, you can search for "Dota 2" and download the video game it's free and very popular.

WORKING FROM HOME AND MAKING TON OF EASY MONEY

You must have heard about online jobs available, like web design, logo design, software development, mobile app development, so on, these are very high paying jobs, a good programmer can demand upto $50 per hour, and he can easily get it.

But programming or technical jobs require technical skills which take time to master and requires lot of study.

But I will tell about jobs which requires you to have very basic computer skills, Facebook skills, email skills and so on, those jobs are called Virtual Assistants jobs, these jobs are very easy to do, anyone can do them.

Employers from USA, Canada hires virtual assistant to assist them in their routine work, pay is minimum $5 per hour, I have Facebook friends who are actually doing it, most of these guys/ girls are from Philippines

Current I have seen spike in hiring for VA in eBook publishing sector, like an author of eBook or eBook publishing company will hire you to assist them in promoting there eBooks

Promoting eBooks means you will be sharing links on Facebook groups or Google+ groups of that author's eBook for people to download and ask for them to review about the eBook on amazon. These reviews are helpful for authors to get feedback and help them get more sales

There is also manipulation going on in Facebook groups about eBook rankings, virtual assistants asks other authors to buy their eBooks and they buy opposite authors eBook, means they both buy each other's eBooks to rank there eBooks higher, more the eBook get sells more it is ranked higher and positive ratings by eBooks purchaser gives it more sales.

Typically an eBooks publishing company or author will pay you to buy eBooks from other authors so they buy their books, it's like a sales swap, you buy mine I will buy yours, and plus eBooks publishers will pay you by the hour. At least $5 per hour to do this basic crappy stuff

How will you get this type of job?, if you want to this type of job, search in Facebook "kindle eBooks", "kindle review swaps", "eBooks review" and so on, after joining this few groups, Facebook will auto suggest you other similar groups, join as many as you can join, I will suggest join all of them, add people into your friends list who are in those groups, now see the postings in the groups, people mostly posting in these groups are virtual assistants, see how they are doing their job, try to understand it.

After observing other VA, then join websites mentioned below

http://www.upwork.com

http://www.fiverr.com

Register on these 2 websites as virtual assistant, check out the profiles of other virtual assistant there, now try to mimic them and make your profile attractive enough to get hired.

This is the world's easiest high paying job

If you are a graphic designer, I will suggest you to join
https://99designs.com/

Currently programmers are also getting hired and paid well online. You can demand $50 per hour; if you are in technology whose skills are very new and fewer programmers available in that skill like Nodejs, Meteor, Ionic framework.

TEACHING ONLINE AND MAKING MONEY (UDEMY MONEY)

I wish I had good voice, I have so much stuff to share, iam working on my voice and soon will be hosting online courses.

There are opportunities for online teaching, and way too much money in it. For example if you want to learn kungfu snake fist style, how will you find the tutor, probably you won't be able to find tutor who can teach you kungfu snake fist style, because the skill is rare and your search will be limited to your local area. But online you can find tutor for almost anything.

I myself taking course on "how to do Rap" from udemy.com, course is good; doing such course will improve my speaking skills and more importantly facing camera skills. Having wide variety of skills helps, it develops new connections in your brain; we need to have variety of skills today in this world to do well. If I can Rap that will be great.

If you have any particular skill, which is useful to others and you can teach it, you can be an instructor at udemy.com

https://www.udemy.com/

You can register as an instructor and teach the whole world online. Money is extremely good in online teaching. I will post you some examples

Check out this course

https://www.udemy.com/the-complete-ios-9-developer-course/

Its only $40, but look at the enrollments this course has
whooping 83,274 students enrolled. Calculate the money this instructor has made, when I

calculated it on the calculator it came to whooping $3330960.

Check out this other course

https://www.udemy.com/advanced-excel/

Training course on excel, and look at the enrollments it got it's more than 72000, and the course is $50, now calculate the amount this instructor has earned.

This is home work for you, calculate the amount this excel instructor has made by starting excel training course on udemy.

You need to be good in the subject you are going to teach, plus you need to have clear voice so that listeners can understand, you need to improve on your voice, there are breathing exercises for that. And voice can be improved with efforts, iam working on my voice.

WRITING EBOOK'S AND MAKING MONEY
(Be the Writer if you can, make money telling stories)

Writers make more than Hollywood actors, and they are not known for money, nobody expects them to be filthy rich, but they are filthy rich.

Check out harry potter writer J.K Rowling, she is filthy rich.

Check out "salman rusdhie", controversy made him rich, he wrote "satanic verses" and all it took him just one book to be filthy rich, although he has death threats, but the money he made and all the beautiful models he married and all the beautiful girls he got laid without marrying, even now at the age of 68+, he Is still getting laid with super models, that kind of life is awesome. I regard Salman Rushdie as a very lucky guy who received direct blessings from his god "Allah", he is living the life of a fukin rock star with all the beautiful girls and money and without disadvantages like unwanted publicity and no privacy, he is like uncle James Bond always gets beautiful girls, Books getting sales and money keep coming.

Previously if you want to publish books you will have to approach a book publishing company and you need to be writer professionally. It was difficult to get your book approved by publishing company, so that they can print and publish it.

Even J.K Rowling stories were rejected numerous times, until one day, daughter of a publisher company read some stories and demanded the whole story, her book was then published but they never thought it could be such a killer sale. You know harry potter movies they are kids' stuff and kids love them, but no one has clear idea which stories may sell or which stories may not. Publishers has to invest money in publishing books, they don't want to publish stories which no one will buy, that's the risk they have to take.

Now with amazon kindle, and Amazon Createspace any one can publish books.

Although there are numerous eBook publishing company like lulu.com, nook and so on but I will focus mainly on amazon kindle, and amazon createspace.

https://kdp.amazon.com/

http://createspace.com/

They both are amazon services, provided to help Authors to publish their books

Kindle publishing is in eBook format, while in createspace you can publish books in paper format

Kindle is pretty straight forward, you can register on kdp.amazon.com and then upload your doc file and set price for your eBook and also decide which part of the world it will be available.

Createspace is print on demand, when you publish story on createspace, it will be available for sale on numerous website and whenever someone orders a copy of your book, it will be printed and then delivered by createspace, it's an amazing service which also has tools to proper format your books, its book cover and all the tools required to help you check how your book will look like after printing.

Another way to sell your eBooks is to convert them into audible format and sell it. It gives you more sales.

Sell it here
http://www.audible.com/

How to sell on audible.com?
In order to publish your audio books on audible.com you need to sign up here

http://www.acx.com/

In that search box, type your eBook title or isbn or your name, it will search from kindle and display it and will ask you to select your eBook, once you select your eBook, it will give you three choices. Like the image shown below

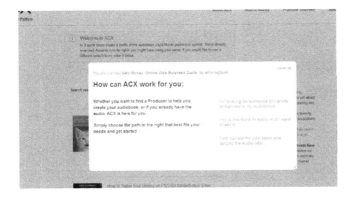

Choose the appropriate choice for you, and move forward for the registration.

The benefit in audible is, if you don't have good voice you can hire a narrator which is available on the website and he will narrate for you, either you can pay in full to the narrator or split your revenue per sell, it's all handled by audible for you.

If you have good voice you can be narrator for many books and get some percentage of per sale for every book of author, this is also good opportunity for people who have good voice, they can lend their voice and make money.

Problem is currently it is only available for only people in USA and UK.

Iam from India, so I cannot publish books on audible, bad for me.

WHAT TYPE OF BOOKS TO WRITE

If you have mastery on a particular subject you can write a book about that, if you want to write a book, write a book on a subject which comes naturally to you. For example if you are good in python programming, you can write a book about that, if you are good in gardening you can write a book about that.

Writing and uploading book on amazon is the first part; next part is selling the book, making people pay for your books. Even if your book is good it is difficult to sale, since at least 30,000 new eBooks are published daily on amazon and your eBook will get lost in clutter, there needs to be a good marketing and advertising technique to sell your eBooks.

There are various ways people are making money on kindle. What some people are doing they are writing eBooks on famous personalities like "Warren Buffet","Mark Zuckerberg", famous sports star, movie star

These eBooks writers are smart guys, they are using leverage of these personalities to sell books like their names, there face on the eBooks, they got nothing to do with those personalities, they are not splitting sales money, they are just using the popularity of these personalities to make money. They search for the information about these personalities on the internet and write 20-50 pages eBook and makes money from it.

Book is judged by its cover by most people, when they see famous personality photo and name they think it's written by them or somewhat related to them and they buy it.

You can use nick names to sell eBooks, you can even use "warren buffet" as nickname, these guys are finding tricks to sell eBooks, I have seen one guy named as author "Socrates" and is using photo of Socrates to sell eBooks, and he is doing well.

People come up with ideas to make money, this is really smart.

Fiction writing sells the most, fiction writing is an art, and you need to make characters which people care about. Just like Television Serials, all hit serials have characters which people care about.

Write sex stories, romance and erotica is the number one niche in eBook sales, people love to read romantic stories, even love with vampires, love with bad guys, romance with billionaire, these type of books sales good.

Sex stories are good to read and will make you horny, few people in the past copied and pasted sex stories available on the internet and made money from it. Copied and paste stories can be easily spotted, amazon has tools for it so don't copy and paste stories.

You can hire someone to write stories for you so that you can sell them on amazon, but the writers who are selling it to you are aware of kindle and they know you can make money from their stories, there prices are very high, and most of the times content is not of good quality, if their stories are good they can write for themselves and sell it on amazon kindle.

One advice, do not buy eBooks whose author details are missing, these books are solely written with intention to make money, there is no quality content in it and they are basically ghost written scripts.

MILLIONAIRES SELLING EBOOK'S
Few people have managed to make millions selling eBooks, iam giving you idea about how some guys have made insane amount of money by writing and publishing books, they are filthy rich, some are richer than Hollywood stars.

Steve Scott

This Guy makes around $30,000-$50,000 per month selling eBooks on kindle

He also publish his income details on his website

http://www.stevescottsite.com/

Amanda Hocking

Amanda Hocking, the 26-year-old paranormal romance writer from Austin, Minnesota, has reportedly become a millionaire by self-publishing on Kindle.

Her writing is good, when I heard about her, I purchased one of her books to see how it is, and she writes good stories.

Over the past 20 months Hocking has sold 1.5m books and made $2.5m, All by herself. Not a single book agent or publishing house or sales force or marketing manager or bookshop anywhere in sight.

Fiction writing is an Art, you need to create characters which everyone cares about, and write a story which will take the reader on an emotional ride.

Stories she writes is an Art, this type of thinking will require lot of free time, you can also develop fiction writing skills by reading lots of fiction novels, lot of authors do that, they read 5-10 books, pick up few ideas from all the books and mix it together and then create their own story. With practice you can develop this skill.

You can check out her website

http://www.worldofamandahocking.com/

Ayaz Menon

Iam jealous of this man, he is making millions writing about sports stars (Cricket players)

He has written one book, it's just that this one book has made him million dollars
The book is

This book was published in 2013, and was in the best seller list since 2013, as of now; even today it is in best seller list in India. This book is getting sales not because of the content, but because of the popularity of that sports star.

To be in amazon best sellers list it should make at least 500-1000 sales per day

It is making 500-1000 sales daily to be able stay in best sellers list.

When I saw it earlier it was just 50 pages, now it is 96 pages; I think author has added more content to it.

I have bought his book; it had nothing special information about Sachin Tendulkar, all that we already know and is available on the internet, it is in the book.

You can check his amazon page and his books

http://www.amazon.in/Ayaz-Memon/e/B00J3F9A7M/ref=dp_byline_cont_book_1

You can easily see for yourself how much money he is making.

Oosh what a lucky guy. He has blessings directly from god to make money easy.

He has also written books on other sports star and they are selling well too.

Robin Sharma

He is the guy who makes millions writing "Holy Sheet" books, the kind of stuff which you already know, like positive thinking, wisdom, great quotes, leadership, and inspiration, the reason why so much depression is there because of these holy sheet books of positive thinking to change your life.

One major quote "Believe in Yourself" is a major cause of depression; everyone believes in themselves, we don't need inspiration guru for that, such quotes gives over confidence to the believers, but when they actually try to do things and achieve something, and when the result greatly varies what they expected, then depression strikes. Failures and repeated failures brings sadness, because they over estimated their ability and tried to do things, failures will make them feel very low in life.

These positive quotes and inspiration like "Be Your own boss", "do what you love" are made to sell eBooks, although sometimes necessary to feel good about ourselves.

There are cases where individuals have done well without putting much effort, but in most case its aptitude and hard work.

Reason why holy gurus have so much power and money, because so many people believe in them, even though they don't have any special powers or anything special about them. They say things which make people feel good about themselves. Leader is the one who says things which people wants to hear.

Attitude and aptitude are two things, attitude is easy and anyone can say inspirational & big things, you can have good attitude within a minute, that's easy anyone can do that.

But real success lays in aptitude your ability to do things, solve problems, aptitude takes time and efforts, and not easy to acquire. That's why we have more big talk and so little actually getting done.

Iam going to write a book about "Holy Sheet", how false notions have become standard, someone lied about it in the past and it's still believed as absolute truth. How consumerism is cleverly imposed on the society and we are chasing things we don't want, we are sold overpriced cars or overpriced fragrance bottle, we buy it because we feel special doing it.

How these holy sheet gurus sells talk, people do not achieve anything even if they follow exact steps and these gurus make money.

I have bought his books, he just stretches what he is going to tell about Art of Living, if the video is about 30 minutes, only 2-3 minutes of content is actually useful, rest is just waste of time. They don't tell you fast straight to the point what's important they stretch it, they stretch it and stretch it.

They charge 1000s of dollars to people for attending there seminars, if they finish their seminars in few minutes, people will want their money back, in order to prove money's worth, they stretch it, and stretch it.

I have read lots of these types of holy sheet books, they don't solve your problems, but they add some wisdom to our thought, I will give you some wisdom here.

To have peaceful and enjoyable life you need to follow some rules, save as much time as you can, save your mental energy as much as you can, exercise and stay fit
have friends who are not very demanding, or else you will waste your time serving their emotional needs. Some individuals are very attention seeking, they demand continuous attention from others, if they are around you they will constantly seek your attention "kick them on the butt", save your attention, attention is a very scarce commodity.

Need to impress others also create unnecessary stress, I keep my hair grey, previously I used to color it. But then I thought why waste time on showing others that you are so young. It doesn't really matter, and people don't really care if you have white hair or black hair. I also saved time which was spent coloring my hairs, my skin also got better. Girls seem to like my white hairs, and it also gives me lot of attention.

World doesn't revolve around us, nobody really cares about the way you look, unless they are planning to marry you.

Iam a programmer turned business person, business requires selling and convincing skills, iam well aware how society and individuals are influenced, influenced to such extent that they chase things which they don't require, they chase them just because others are buying it, how artificial demand is created to push sales, how individuals are tricked to chase things which are in plenty but artificial shortage is created to push price and customer buying it to feel special even when there is nothing special about it.

A typical Joe is always looking for something which will make him feel special. He will buy expensive iPhone just to show his colleagues how cool he is, how he can afford such a costly phone. This kind of showoff creates unnecessary stress. You buy things which you cannot afford and creates debt, and nobody really cares you have iPhone.

An emotional need to feel special about ourselves is actually adding more stress.

It's all mind game make them feel special, push sales, after all companies has to sell every day to make profits and pay salaries.

Apple has exploited this tendency to maximum extent they make people wait, stand in-line to purchase their products, and people gladly do it. They create such artificial hype by limiting the units to be sold. Why there are diehard fans for apple products?, because the customer has chosen them, they were not sold the product; they took efforts to buy it & invested in it.
Even if you offer better alternative for apple with a lower price still fans won't buy it, because they have made the decision and they want to stay consistent with it, how can

they be wrong. I have iPhone 6+, it has some good features, but the price is way too high for those features, it's not actually value for money. People don't want to accept they were wrong.

There is a technique where you don't sell them goods; they queue to buy your goods. This is achieved by limiting supply and using celebrities to promote their brands. Apple does this all the time, and there celebrity was "Steve Jobs". "Steve jobs" was regular consumer of "LSD", I have heard that LSD gives self-realization, and adds to your wisdom, but LSD can also be reason for him having cancer.

Sell books with information which people already aware of, most people are searching for confirmation not information, "that is well explained in blogging money", sell them holy sheet inspirational quotes, tell them how to improve their life, tell them how to stay healthy in life even when they themselves are suffering from diabetes. Tell them how they can earn millions of dollars and still have plenty of time to spend with family.

I learned 2 useful advices after watching 2 hours of his video, the advice I will give you, to save time automate things like use tools like todoist, https://ifttt.com.

Delegate things (hire someone to do your repetitive task), look I saved your 2 hours of time, by straightly telling you 2 important points.

This is American dream, lots of money with lots of free time. You can reduce your mental energy by setting reminders so that you don't have to remember things that ease some of your mental load. You can buy "Amazon Echo" that will be lot of help, we need lot of smart "AI", robots to free ourselves from daily chores, time is a limited resource focus should be on saving time.

You can save time by reducing to watch news, you just need to be aware of what's happening around you, just not get too aware of it, news channel brings in lot of negativity and you end up wasting your mental energy on things which you cannot control like criticizing political situation, even sports is a time waster and you end up wasting mental energy in appreciating or criticizing sports person. have a private mobile phone don't give that number to anybody not even family, use it just for reminders, switch off all your other mobile phones, mobile phones is the biggest distraction, when you are working on something important, a single whatsup message beep will disturb you, it is estimated that employees waste at least 3 hours daily at work place because of mobile phones. When someone is in middle of something and he gets distracted by email or mobile ring, when he returns back to work, he has to think "Where was he, What was he doing" that wastes some time in starting up work again. Average person checks his mobile at least 200+ times every day see how much time he wastes doing nothing.

Switch of your cell phone, it will give you peace of mind, I do it many times, it helps me reduce clutter in my brain I get enough space to think and focus on things which I want to do, and not get distracted. Some people have got peace of mind after deleting there Facebook account. Facebook is also a big time waster, but you have your friends there & you may develop valuable connections.

Key here is to save as much time & mental energy possible, so that you have that mental space to be more creative, enough mental space to think on things which matters.

Lot of people whom I observed "average Joes", waste times in discussing what they eat, what they wear, they say it in such away as if they have done something great, like went to Mars and came back. Human is a social animal and people find happiness in small things, but that cuts our energy from the tasks which matters the most and is directed to the tasks which don't matter at all. Joes also waste lot of time and mental energy on discussing about celebrities.

Most of the people are unsure about why problems are happening in their life, because they are too occupied, busy discussing about sports events, sports star, celebrities & about their friends. They have drained all there mental energy and cluttered their brain, there is no space available in the brain to think about the cause of problems in their lives. They simply cannot figure it out.

Reason why these motivational speakers are making money, because society is changing at a very rapid pace and people are not sure what to do next, they are looking for answers or why sudden bad things happening in their life, Stress is actually your inability to handle or control the situation for ex some people get stressed when other person is driving the car fast, reason why?, It is not question of trust actually it's the person who is not sitting on the driver's seat feels that he is not in control of the situation that brings him stress.

today's age is information age, you got to constantly update yourself, you need to have more cognitive skills, have to quickly learn new things, for example why students (higher studies) are stressed, because there are so many subjects and the volume of information is large, they got to consume that large volume of information to pass tests, which requires long hours of study it is difficult to do, because after few hours brains stop taking information even though you are forcing your brain to take it, but brain simply don't want any more information.

Being in IT industry I myself have to study lot of technologies try them out and see for myself which works best. It requires long hours of study

People should figure out what the root cause of a bad thing happening to them, most of the time they are unsure from where this bad luck is coming, for example I was earning huge money from a jobsite somewhere around in 2005-2007, money was coming in plenty and I was having a good life, I was hardly working or studying but still getting plenty of money, then all of a sudden money supply got lessen then there where started bad things happening, when the revenue dropped problems started coming, now you see here what the problem was?, problem was I was not making enough money because my jobsite had got outdated technology wise and my old marketing techniques were not working, many better jobsites have sprang up with the technologies and features I was not aware of. To have jobsite better than the competition I will have to upgrade with the latest technologies and come up with marketing strategy that works what technologies to study iam not aware of. To better understanding what technology and design serve my purpose, I had to study wide range of technologies so that I can compare and differentiate and decide what is more appropriate for me, now imagine how much time it will take to study so many technologies and master enough to implement, understand the stress here, study and implement or you will be out of business with no money, when things change and you suffer that brings stress, now only real solution for my stress is actually having some other business or idea which can make me good enough money or upgrade my existing jobsite with technologies and new marketing strategy which works. The real solution for my problem is good income source; big drop in income source has allowed problems to occur, none of these motivational gurus have problems to my solutions and many other peoples problem, when people are confused and are not sure what's causing problems in their life, its then these common people buy motivational gurus stuff, which hardly helps.

Problem of stress is actually rapidly changing situations around us, and we are just not well versed with it, not sure what to do, and also demand for high cognitive skills. When you spend years mastering some skillset and later find out that skillset is no longer required, you have to master another skillset that puts enormous pressure on your brain. Learning is lot of hard work.

When 3D Printers become a normal industry standard for producing factory goods, the people who spent years mastering a particular skillset to produce a particular product will luse their jobs, and that will put immense pressure on them. If that factory worker is too busy in his life, too busy with family chores, too busy in sports, he won't be able to figure out his problem source, just because he was too occupied.

Motivational gurus have no solutions to your problems; they can add wisdom which may help.

If someone is suffering from cancer and facing lot of problems in life, it's because of the disease which has brought lot of problems with it, his inability to work, he needs people around to take care of himself. Income has gone down, you see problem here is cancer, nothing will change, and problems will only continue to increase until his cancer is fixed. This is something to be worry about; stress will naturally occur to him and his family. Motivational gurus cannot solve this person's problem; they only have inspirational stories and quotes.

Things around us will change continuously; we have no control over it. But we can save our mental space by not filling it with unnecessary things which don't matter, that will help us have enough space in brain to figure out the cause of the problem and think solution for it.

Robert T. Kiyosaki

He is the guy who has made millions, and still making millions just by writing and selling one book "Rich Dad Poor Dad", this guy is actually a genius, he served in American army and was posted as captain in Vietnam, after he left army, he joined Xerox Corporation, and was in top 5 sales person, most of the time number 1 in sales. Sales are difficult to get and staying number one for 5 years requires some special talent, which he has proved. He is also good speaker, I have seen him talk in Oprah Winfrey show, he is kinda smart person

I have read his book, he says about be your own boss, he recommend network marketing (MLM), to be quick rich

Everybody will like to be their own boss, but not everyone can do it, he wrote a book about everybody's need and see he is a super millionaire.

He wrote this book in the year 1997, and it is still in best seller list. Imagine how much this guy is making.

Now this is homework for you "calculate how much money Robert Kiyosaki is making".

J AMES P ATTERSON

James Brendan Patterson is an American author. He is largely known for his novels about fictional psychologist Alex Cross.

He tops Forbes rich authors list, his net worth is around $94 million dollars.

Check out his website

http://www.jamespatterson.com/

STEPHEN KING

This guy writes horror books, and makes money selling them

You can check out his website

http://stephenking.com/

Making Money with Windows Azure

Windows azure is a cloud service from Microsoft, you can build Api or services which can help other people in their Apps.

For example Country, State, City list service

You can provide a service which can give clients countries, states and city list. If a company is a making a website it will have registration form, that registration form will also have country, state, and city input fields

In order to populate this fields, that company either have to enter country, state, city data into their database or use a service which can provide those data.

This type of service is already available in azure, it also gives list of states based on the country selected, city list according to the state selected, it also give pin number and so on.

Are you aware of Google maps service, they provide city name and location details about the user to website based on users geo coordinates, that's a service which other website owners use and they pay per transaction, every 1000 transaction or every 10,000 transaction.

There are various Api and services available on Azure, and they charge per transaction

There is a huge scope of revenue here, but its very technical to build services or Api to be used for technical people, basically you are going to provide Api or service which can be used for other projects.

There are face detecting Api, IOT services Api on windows azure, you can build similar thing, something unique and can charge people for using your services.

What azure provides is the computing power for your application or service, millions of computer processing power is available.

Azure is a very technical beast; you can earn money by providing consulting service to people who wants to move to azure cloud. Like configuring there app environment and tweaking there app for windows azure.

Sell and implement windows365 to your clients, or monitoring your clients Azure cloud.

You can also use services which are already available on windows azure, that speeds up your project, some of the services available are highly technical in nature, you will have hard time developing them, so instead use those services. save time.

I know one programmer personally he makes lot of money by creating services for salesforce.com, which iam covering salesforce chapter.

Making Money with Salesforce.com

Salesforce.com is very easy cow to milk, all major companies use salesforce.com for marketing, Google use it, Apple uses it, and so all the others.

Currently there is huge demand for sales force a developer, money is very good and severe shortage of programmers.

When I heard lot of people are making money developing services or apis or developing apps or being handy man for your clients, managing there salesforce automation. I checked about programming skills required for the job, 90% of cases you won't be required to code, all the tools required for the job are already built in, you just needs to know how to use them. Coding in salesforce.com is very easy. I have checked the landscape and in no time you will be able to learn it.

Sales force automation landscape has two options 1st "declarative tools" point and click no coding required.

2nd option Coding Tools, understand the tools learn them, understand the syntax, when and where at which point to apply.

In the 2nd option coding tools there is front end and backend, front end for users to interact uses "visualforce", "lightening" as programming language

And at backend there is" Apex Triggers, Apex Classes, SOQL". SOQL (salesforce object query language) is almost like SQL programming language; in apex triggers and classes you are going to use SOQL

You can join salesforce.com developers group and learn more about salesforce api and services

https://developer.salesforce.com/

There are online editors to code in salesforce.com or you can use IDE provided by salesforce.com

Or download sublimetext

https://www.sublimetext.com/

You can use submlimetext as your editor and install a plugin mavinsmate

http://mavensmate.com/

sublimetext with mavinsmate plugin is preferred and recommended way to develop salesforce apps

Minimum salary you can expect as salesforce developer is around $150,000 per anum.

BLOGGING MONEY

Iam a programmer, content writing is not my skill, but when I saw huge revenues of blog, very huge, it got my attention. These blogs had nothing special about them, those blogs were kind of basic, anyone can make them, they don't require any technical skills, no learning Curve, but the revenue was awesome.

Creating a website and maintaining it requires technical skills and money, while maintaining a blog is extremely easy and don't require much cost or technical skills, blogs can be free in most cases. Some blogs have revenue more than high traffic websites. Many bloggers have built empires from just one blog.

For example

http://www.buzzfeed.com

This blog is valued over $1 billion, it's just a simple blog, but it has interesting content for everyone. But buzzfeed.com is slightly technical, they use surveys to gather information of the user, and then show content which is more relevant to him. For example a man from Texas visits buzzfeed.com, website will show exciting content which is more linked to him, for example Texas jokes, amazing Texas happening, and so on. Basically it tailors content according to the users.

HOW TO INCREASE SOCIAL SHARING (MASTER THE ART OF GETTING YOUR CONTENT SHARED).

There is a reason why certain people share certain posts, how to make your posts get more shares, I will explain. Most people on the internet are searching for confirmation, rather than information, they believe in certain idea and search for proof which supports there notions, for example a radical Muslim will search all over internet to support his claim that Muslims are suffering and he needs to do something, he will search for the atrocity pictures, he will search for Palestine problem, he will search for hate speeches of their enemies, they will find all the evidence which supports their ideas and then that content they will share on their social networks.

I met many Muslims online, they say the same thing like radical Muslims, they all seem to support "Sharia Law" except they are non-violent, they will tell few verses from Quran to show how Islam is very peaceful and nonviolent and everything is just a west conspiracy, they just completely deny overwhelming evidence which is right before their own eyes, they live in their own bubble.

They all seem to agree that women should be covered from head to toe, that is to please "Allah", even educated Muslims agree to this notion, they will show you some Quran verses, how women can be saved from rape, west has highest number of rapes, because women there don't wear veils. Check out there Facebook profiles, they all seem to agree on the same thing.

Trick to get your content more shared, target some specific stereotypes, for ex if you have lot of Muslim followers post an article how Veil is good for women, you will notice lot of Muslims will share your blog post on their walls, literally its free advertising.

It's not a question about being right or wrong; it's a question about marketing, you will have to write articles on your blog, which specific type of people agree upon. You only speak to your own tribe. Learn from politicians how they speak for only certain type of people. That's there market they know how to keep it.

1000s of examples are available for everything, you just need to pick that up at the right time, for example failed student will always pick examples to show that how failed students are successful in life, they will just pick up few exceptional students examples who failed and later made big. Media exaggerates exceptions that give them lot of attention. Blow them out of proportion and increase their TRP.

Everybody thinks they are always right.

Every person stays in his own bubble they have their own ideas about how the world works, and they are constantly looking for information which supports their notions.

Attention grabbing is the toughest part, when a user notices something that relates to him, he immediately gives his attention to it. That's the key to get your content to be shared and to be more liked. You got to support users notions and give evidence to support it, well that's difficult to guess, buzzfeed uses surveys to analyses user and show according to his tastes, for example a Texan user will share the content which supports his idea about Texan which will make Texan look good, he will share that on his social network wall, and his friends most likely to be Texan they will again re-share on their wall, that's how it gets viral and lot of traffic is generated.

People share and like content which supports there notion or if it makes them look good among others, or if it makes them appear intelligent to others.

Buzzfeed.com is little technical they are using big data to analyze users and finding more ways to know more about users and show content according to them.

I just gave you an example on how huge money can be made just from blog, although buzzfeed is bit technical but it's still not that technical as Google, Facebook. A guy with little above average skills on big data and web technologies can start blog similar to buzzfeed.com with very little hosting cost. But starting service like Google is difficult, Google revenue is justified because the skills they have, no other tech giants have managed to duplicate it, Microsoft still struggles, yahoo is looking for buyers.

WHY I PAID ATTENTION TO BLOGGING

Starting a web service which can make you lot of money is difficult and requires lot of technical skills, iam a technical guy but the time and effort it takes to start a technical service is enormous.

That's why I paid attention to blogging and found ways to make revenue from it, iam telling you the same exact technique which I used.

Key to blogging revenue is you have authority on a particular subject or you have large following of subscribers to your blog, SEO thingy and keyword optimization doesn't work, it worked in the past now it doesn't, now it is relevancy which I will discuss further.

To have an authority on a particular subject you need to study and master that particular subject, which is actually hard work, which few can do, if you can do it, there is lot of money in that too.

When you have authority on a particular subject, when someone does Google search about it, your blog appears in the search result and you get traffic. They also subscribe to your blog if your subject matter, matters to them.

Another way is "Generalized Blogging" to have a Facebook page, community, Google+ page or profile and have large following for it, and you share your blog post to these large followers and get traffic to your blog and make money.

Key to this type of blogging revenue is the bucket; bucket means the bucket of people who are following you, more the followers you have more the money you can make

Here in this eBook, I will be mostly talking about generalized types of blogs which doesn't require authority on a particular subject, the blogs which are basic but key here is large number of followers to which you are going to share your blog post.

I will be telling you trick to have large followers to your profile, and then sharing the blog post to that profile and getting lot of traffic to your blog post.

Trick is to share awesome YouTube videos on your BlogSpot or posting some attention grabbing content on your blog and then sharing that blog post on your social network, where you have large followers.

For example

Boredpanda.com worth $97 million

ad revenue is about $50,000 per day

see their Facebook following

https://www.facebook.com/boredpanda/?fref=ts

rajnikantvscidjokes.in worth $47 million

daily advertisement revenue is around $10,000 per day

See their Facebook following

https://www.facebook.com/Rajnikant.Vs.CIDJokez/?fref=ts

These types of blogs are valued in millions not because these blogs have some earth shattering stuff in them, but because they have a large, very large following. A simple blog post share brings lot of traffic to their blogs.

I myself tried blogging and made money from it.

I will show you how I created profiles and got large followings, and shared my blog post to them and earned 1000s of dollars, I will be explaining the same strategy in this eBook

I have created over 50+ profiles on Google+ and have over 20,000 followers for each profile, one profile I created have over 127000 followers. This is the key trick to traffic, more the followers you have more the traffic and more the money.

I will also tell you, how I created network of profiles by adding each other, so more people add my profiles and my blog post become highly relevant to them. When you add all your profiles to each other, Google+ suggest all your other profiles as well to these users, for example if you have 2 profiles A and B both adding each other, when Mr. X adds your profile A to his friends list then Google+ will also suggest profile B to Mr. X, since profile A is having B in his friends list, that way he will add both of your profiles, and your content will become more relevant to Mr. X. when Mr. X adds your profile, his friends are also alerted and they also add you in their profile, then their friends are alerted, this cycle goes on.

☐ INTRODUCTION To Blogging

Most successful blogger had no idea, that they could make money blogging, they accidentally got into blogging and got rich.

Quote by

"shivanand baba Shivyogi""Lot of good things happens by accident"

Before getting into web business I was a programmer, I started websites with no idea about how to make money from it, then AdSense and affiliate programs came into existence and my websites started making money. "You see accident here"

You came across my eBook and purchased it, that also might be an accident, so be hopeful.

A blog is basically a journal that is available on the web. The activity of updating a blog is "blogging" and someone who keeps a blog is a "blogger."

It's like writing and keeping a dairy.

In this eBook, I will give you sure shot technique which I used myself, to make money from blog, I have made over $1000 from a single blog post, I will also show you my blog and the communities I made to promote these blogs, how I got lot of followers. And still make auto money from these blogs, even when I don't update them.

I will explain you design strategy and promotion strategy

Although they are many blogging scripts, WordPress the most popular, but we will be using blogger.com as our blogging platform. □

HOW TO START A BLOG.

To start a blog is basically easy, there are many blogging scripts are available for free, and there are also paid scripts, you can download them and host it, but in this eBook iam going to use http://www.blogger.com , why blogger?, its owned by Google, its free, easy to setup and can be started instantly

Most successful bloggers are using WordPress; WordPress blog will allow you more control with more features

But WordPress is little technical to setup, you will incur hosting cost, while blogger.com is free, you can even host your own custom domain on blogger.com

Some of the free blogging software available

1. Wordpress

2. Jhoomla

3. Drupal

4. Nineblog

5. Ghost

6. Plone

There are many more, but the above list is sufficient enough

Some of the paid blogging scripts available "STIVA Blog Script"

There are many paid blogging scripts, but they don't offer any significant benefits to purchase and use them, when all the needed features are there in free blog scripts, who will pay for blogging scripts.

All these blogs are Php MySQL scripts; I had difficult time managing them.

Even though they are preconfigured, and come with lot of free modules, but still you will have hard time configuring it. It is quite technical to use them.

That's why we will be using blogger; it's free and very easy to use.

BLOGGING DESIGN STRATEGY AND TEMPLATES

Now as I mentioned earlier that we are going to use blogger.com as our blogging platform, reason no hosting cost and ease of use.

Go signup here

http://www.blogger.com

it is basically self-explainer, after signing up you click on "new blog" option then it will ask you to name your blog, you name it, use the words in name which represent your blog, then it will ask you to choose template, you select one and then create, oosh, blog will be created.

If you have AdSense account, you can link it to your blogger account and show ads. Recently AdSense have become strict, in approving ads to your blog, you need to have enough natural traffic and content of your blog must be good enough.

In order to show AdSense ads to your blog, you will have to use special templates, Google won't allow you to show AdSense ads if you are using basic templates provided by blogger

I recommend you to go here

http://newbloggerthemes.com/

It has plenty of free templates you can use, download them and install them, it also has installation instructions, and it is pretty straight forward.

You can also do Google search for templates for blogger.com,

Do some sample posts; make sure your blog is good looking.

BLOG DESIGN

ADD GOOGLE+ PROFILE
Add your Google+ profile on the side bar, it helps in getting more followers to your profile and it makes your blog look trust worthy.

ADD FEEDBURNER
In the layout section of the blogger.com, you will have the widget "Follow by email" which you can use, use it. Place that widget in the side bar. It is a feedburner which lets subscribe to your feed, that is when a user decides to follow your blog, he add his email in "follow by email" option, and whenever you add new posts to your blog, that user will get email.

This option is necessary so that you get regular readers for your blog.

You can also use paid auto responders, but if your revenue is from Google ads or another ads, it's not worth it. Because the paid auto responders are costly

Check their pricing

http://www.mailchimp.com

http://www.getresponse.com

If you check their pricing it is costly, unless you are selling some product, those auto responders are not worthy, these auto responders service are mostly used by mlm marketing guys, because they are selling membership, they can afford it.

But when your blog revenue is from Google Ads or any other Ads, you will need very large following, so it's better to use feed burner a free auto responder which will auto manage your subscribers.

Put a link of your blog Facebook or Google fan page on the blog, so users can follow your Facebook and Google+ page

FEEDBURNER DESIGN STRATEGY

Feedburner will mail all your content in email, the entire post by default, that means if you write a single post on your blog, that entire blog post will be emailed to the subscribers, which you don't want. What you want is user click on the link and visits your blog to read that post. Because that's what is gona make you money.

You will have to manage the content users receive.

Visit this page

http://feedburner.google.com/

Login with email account, which you are using for blogger, after login it, will take you to this page.

https://feedburner.google.com/fb/a/myfeeds

This page will show you all the feed titles with total number of subscribers for each feed, feed title will be your blog title.

You can click on the feed title and manage content and subscribers to this feed.

After clicking that it will take to the page where you can manage, there will be four tabs, "Analyze", "Optimize", "Publicize", "troubleshootize".

Click on the optimize tab, at the end on the left side menu, you will see the option "Summary Burner" , click on that.

In this option you can limit the content which is emailed to the subscriber, use 100 or 200, this is the most required feature you need.

There are many other features which you can check it out.

AUTHORITY BLOGGING

When you have mastery in particular field or you are some kinda celebrity you can do authority blogging

People loves celebrities and subscribe to their blogs, you who downloaded my eBook is most likely not a celebrity so you won't be having that kind of following

Programmers have advantage here, if you are a programmer, you can have a blog about programming, for ex. If you are asp.net programmer, you can write articles about asp.net features, addons, how-to stuff, you can write about errors you got and how you fixed it, this works the most, many programmers comes across variety of programming errors every day and they do Google search for it. If your blog has that error solution your blog page will be shown to the Google searcher, he will visit to your blog and mostly likely will also subscribe to your blog and add you in his friends list.

There are many individuals who have successfully done it

Examples of successful authority blogging

PINAL DAVE
he is an Ms-sql server guy, he works full time on Ms-sql server, what he did was he wrote all the errors he got and solutions he found on a blog, to keep records of it, so that if in future such thing reoccurs he can go to the blog and refer back. He started to notice that they were

many visitors to his blog; the other Ms-sql developers who had similar kind of problem used Google to search for the problem solution and found his blog. He is quite famous in SQL world

Look at his website

http://blog.sqlauthority.com/

His blog is worth $2 million and makes over $1200 per day from AdSense advertising, that's good, he earns from blogging than his job salary.

This type of money is good, since there is no investment cost at all, no staff to pay; only investment is his knowledge.

SRINIVAS TAMADA
Srinivas Tamada is a Chennai based blogger. His blog is about programming, Ajax, PHP and other web design aspect. Hence, the blog is for people that are more technical rather a non-professional. His blog is 9lessons.info and

very popular among developer & programmer community. His income is around $30,000-$40,000 per month from AdSense Ads, his blog is valued around $2 million.

His blog is

http://www.9lessons.info

You can see its .info domain not even .com, still his website is famous, because the authority he has on a particular topic Php, MySQL and web design. Coding is his bread and butter, he just blog about what he knows and also make money from it, again there is absolutely no investment cost here, he just blogs what he knows.

MISS MALINI

Miss malini is a celebrity blogger, her blog is missmalini.com, she started her career as a radio jockey, she was also head of digital content for Channel V

Her blog gives fashion tips; the blogs niche is fashion and celebrity. I personally met missmalini.com team, they travel by air plane to every celebrity event, takes photographs with them, talk to them. Her blog is valued around $ 28 million dollars, but I don't think they are making revenue via ads, since they have huge variable cost, their travel by airplane for every celebrity, fashion events, stays in 5 star hotels, that's a high cost; it also has staff, which again is a cost. Unless Miss Malini is selling some high-end stuff like designer bags, designer dress, she is losing money, she started this blog because she is well versed with show business that's why she started missmalini.com.

You can see her Facebook page and Google+ page has very large following, but don't get misled by that, 90% of these people are not interested in her fashion stuff, they just added her because she is a lady, they want to do friendship with her.

Her blog
http://www.missmalini.com

KATIE, THE "WELLNESS MAMA"

Her blog
http://wellnessmama.com/

The blog is designed taking moms into consideration; overall the blog is about health and wellness. She give healthy cooking tips, tips of solutions for common health related problems, she has massive followers and when you search internet for health related tips, her blog appears.

You see the few examples of successful people I have stated, started their blog, because they were masters in their own field, and they shared their information with others and got paid via ads or selling some stuff, that's what is called authority blogging.

If you are well versed with particular subject, you can start a blog about that.

GENERALIZED BLOGGING
When you don't have an authority on any particular topic, you are just an average Joe;

you can do generalized blogging and still make money

I myself have made 1000s of dollars from generalized blogging, it's easy, you write some interesting content which you can get from internet search, read it and modify it and post it in your blog, do not copy and paste content on your blog, it can easily be found out, and your AdSense account may get disabled by that, or Google might disable showing ads on that blog.

This single post alone got me over $1000

http://tanyasharm.blogspot.in/2015/09/superb-belly-dance-watch-out-this-video.html

Check the likes it has 1678+ and it was shared by many Google+ users. Blogging theme is not displaying the shares it got.

You can easily see there is nothing in that post, only a girl dancing but I was able to bring massive traffic to it, because girl pic is what makes people click. I shared this post on profiles I created, and also to YouTube G+ communities.

Sharing your blog post on G+ communities bring massive traffic, but you only share to those communities which have large number of members, share blog post on 1 or 2 max. If you share the same blog post to many other communities, it will be marked as spam and won't be visible to other community members.

Share your blog post only to the relevant community, if your blog post is about skin, then post it only in skin related community, that too only 1 or 2 max communities

For example
check out my generalized blog
http://jokesnfunblog.blogspot.in/ (this blog made me somewhat money, but I have abandoned it)

http://tanyasharm.blogspot.in/ ←- this blog made me 1000s of dollars

Check out the profiles I made to get traffic to these blogs

For safety and security of mine, Iam just going to show you just two fake profiles i made for getting traffic

https://plus.google.com/104537595517021124201

(Over 51000 followers)

https://plus.google.com/u/0/107746096494050048315/posts

(Over 127000 followers)

I have actually made around 50 fake profiles of beautiful girls and added them to each other, for example if you have profile a, b, c, d, e, f make sure all your profiles add each other, so it becomes a friends network, when someone adds your profile a, Google+ will suggest him profile b, c, d, e, f and also his friends will be notified, so they add your profile as well.

Many people are doing it, and they generate massive income via it.

Check this out

https://plus.google.com/+PriyankaNath

Look at her followers 1,786,115 followers, when I saw it

https://plus.google.com/+AasitaKhan

Over 450,000 followers

https://plus.google.com/111094079788389654396

1,151,448 followers when I saw it

Iam very sure it's a guy who is behind these profiles.

Such a huge bucket of followers one can easily generate revenue of over $1000 per day, just by sharing a blog post, you can see how many likes, shares their posts get.

They make such profiles either to get traffic to their blogs or promote some website.

Some of communities I created for traffic generation

https://plus.google.com/communities/108084055090402568074

(Over 23000 members)

https://plus.google.com/communities/1122929
98400758801962

(Over 25000 members)

How to have large number of followers

The key to generalized blogging success is
followers, you need to have big bucket of
followers to generate kind of traffic to make
money.

FACEBOOK STRATEGY

Getting large number of followers on Facebook
is difficult if you make a fake profile of a
beautiful girl and accepts several friends
request in a short time, they are most likely to
suspend your account, until you submit some
documents.

So do not fake profile, make a profile page
with beautiful girl in it, it does look like profile

but it only has like button, no add as a friend button, so lot of users will like your page.

Facebook will suspend your profile if all of a sudden you get and you accept too many friend requests. Make Facebook page instead

I got my several of Facebook account banned, with large followings in it, that was the sad part since I invested so much time and energy doing it and all of sudden they were gone.

GOOGLE+ STRATEGY

Google+ is also very strict but not as strict as Facebook, you can use Google+ to create large following, and most of the traffic I got is from Google+.

Remember Google+ also suspends your profile, if you do too much website sharing on your Google+ profile it will most likely get banned. I also got few of my profiles banned in Google+

Google+ dislikes external website pasting in the post sharing, they are ok with blogger.com shares

Basically create profiles of beautiful girls, if possible hire beautiful girls, add all your profiles to each other, suppose if you make profile a, b, c, d then profile a should b, c, d , I mean all the profile should add each other.

then join communities in Google+ of dating, friendship, YouTube or groups which have large number of members, when you join them just post "hi, hello", when people see beautiful girls pic, they will add you, once they add you their friends will be notified and they most likely will add you as well, here cycle of adding your profile gets started, try this you will at least have 100 followers in a day just by doing it 1-2 hours.

In the initial stages like and share content of other members who are posting in that group

ATTENTION GRABBING CONTENT

Attention is very scarce in today's world as too much information is available for an average person to grasp

Attention grabbing is an art & science; a human can give attention to only one thing at a time. And we want his attention on our post.

Humans are evolved to pay attention the most to the life threatening situation, like a gun firing, huge blast, they will naturally pay immediate attention to it, since its life threatening situation.

But here we are not going to do bomb blast to get immediate attention of people.

Pictures of animal fighting, abnormal things, pictures of beautiful women, title with something out of ordinary, sex gossips of celebrities, nude photos, injustice, celebrity photos, Kayne West, Kim Kadarshini these are few examples of which people pay more attention.

If you are regular user of Facebook, you must have come across several attention grabbing posts and pictures.

You need to have an attention grabbing title and an image for your blog post.

For example check out few of our blog posts

http://tanyasharm.blogspot.in/2016/02/5-most-beautiful-criminals-in-world.html

Title "Most Beautiful Criminals in the World"

http://tanyasharm.blogspot.in/2016/02/girl-has-spent-14000-to-look-like.html

Title "GIRL HAS SPENT $14,000 TO LOOK LIKE DISNEY PRINCESSES"

http://tanyasharm.blogspot.in/2016/02/girl-has-spent-14000-to-look-like.html

Title "You have the guts to do that?"

http://tanyasharm.blogspot.in/2016/02/you-have-guts-to-do-that.html

here it is a special case, we have developed a gif image of this video and posted at the bottom of the blog post, since when the blog post is shared in Facebook or Google+ that gif image will appear and it will show half the stunt, to see the full stunt user has to click on the image and visit our blog.

Sharing exciting videos from YouTube is good way to increase traffic to your blog; you just have to search for exciting videos in YouTube and write just 1 or 2 sentences about it and post it. That's super easy

You can share movie trailers; they are action packed and bring lot of traffic

Check this out

http://tanyasharm.blogspot.in/2016/02/watch-brand-new-trailer-for-disneys.html

you can easily see the post has video first and few sentences later, that's because nobody gona read those sentences but only watch videos, that's just a description we provide. At the bottom of the page you have noticed an image of YouTube video content, that image was created using print screen and then that "> play" icon added to this image via Photoshop.

That image is specially created for sharing on Facebook, and Google+, when users see that image they click on that image to play, thinking it's a video; they are redirected to our website, where they can see the video. This is how you can make visitors visit on your website.

Lot many are using this technique, especially these two

https://www.facebook.com/Esquire/?fref=ts

https://www.facebook.com/YaBoyKhalilUnderwood/?fref=ts

SHARING YOUR CONTENT

Join Google+ communities, if your content is about hair color, you can join communities related to hair and you can share your content there, remember share your content only in communities which relate to your content, for example if you have hair related content and you share it Google+ car related community, your content will automatically get into spam and that community admin or moderator may ban you.

Most communities won't approve your content, unless you provide some benefits to that community. What they expect is you comment on their community content, share it, like it. You need to be active member in the community. If they see you regular contributing, they will approve all your posts.

Many communities are not moderated you can post there, but be aware if you share the same content in different communities your content will most likely be marked as spam and won't appear in the community, it will appear to you and your friends but it won't appear to other members of the community.

Create your own community with subject related to love, romance, fun. Invite your friends, post some content on it.

You will find lot of unique and interesting photos, quotes on the internet post those quotes in your community, your community need to have content.

RELEVANCY AND SEO

Seo is no more keywords and your page title, it is more about what is relevant to the user, suppose if a user types "temperature" in Google search, he will get to see his current city temperature, Google knows your city and thinks you are looking for temperature of your current city.

If you type temperature and you are situated in Delhi, it will show Delhi temperature, if you are situated in Bangalore it will show Bangalore temperature.

That's relevancy

For example if your friend is using a particular website for shopping, when you are interested in shopping and does a Google search for it, it will show you website which your friend is using, since he is your friend and he is using particular website, that website has become more relevant to you.

Facebook also uses relevancy to a major extent, if you have Facebook friend with whom you have chatted and wished on his birthday, Facebook knows he is more relevant to you, Facebook will auto suggest Facebook groups and friends of the person with whom you have interacted more often.

If your Facebook friends with whom you have interacted joins a Facebook group, Facebook will suggest you that group.

If large number of people adds you in their friendliest if you share your blog post on your wall, that website or blog becomes more relevant to your followers.

Getting AdSense Account Approved for your blog

If your AdSense account is not getting approved then you can try this

https://www.exoclick.com/

It is not as good as AdSense, but they also pay; you can search for alternatives for AdSense on Google

In the past, getting AdSense approved was very easy, simple website and your account got approved, but they have restricted entry into their AdSense program. They require quality website with natural traffic to get approved for their program

Few steps iam explaining below

High Quality Blog Post

You need at least 40 blog post of good quality content before you apply for the program, do it before you apply
keep you content focus on a macro niche, why iam saying macro niche, if you limit your blog content to only one particular subject Google thinks that you are creating a spam domain around it to rank higher.

Do not copy and paste content from other websites, not even a single sentence, Google panda algorithm easily detects copy and paste, for that only panda algorithm was made.

PROHIBITED WEBSITE NICHES
do not have sex related content, porn, drugs related content on your website, hacking cracking also No no.
no multi-level programs, and work from home jobs content. No alcohol related content

NO THIRD PARTY ADS
before applying to AdSense make sure you don't allow or place any other third party banner ad code on your website.
Do not have affiliate links on your blog. Your blog is about information not sales pitch.

WEBSITE DESIGN AND USER EXPERIENCE
Use special templates for blog; you can search for free blogger templates in Google. If you use basic templates provided by blogger, your account won't get approved.

You can try this website
http://newbloggerthemes.com/

Plenty of free themes available.

IMPORTANT PAGES:

Google wants to know your identity before you sign up to their AdSense program. So make sure you create the following pages on your website as soon as possible.

- Privacy Policy
- Disclaimer Policy
- Terms of Usage
- Contact Us

About Us (Write your name and address through which you applied the AdSense account)

In the about us section, clearly mention who you are, and why is this website made for, what is the benefit people get out of your website. The clearer, more better the chances of your approval. Keep your spelling mistakes, grammar and punctuation clear when you do this.

TIME SAVING TOOLS

If you can hire someone to do your repetitive tasks, even though you will have to pay salary, it is still a sweet deal
time is fixed for everyone, you can earn more money, but you cannot earn more time.

Do shopping via online website, you save time avoiding traffic and going through the stores, checking the products and then sometimes bargaining.

Avoid friends or relatives who are very demanding, you complete their one demand, then comes the other, you will have queue of demands and you will get busy fulfilling their demands & taking care of their feelings. Big No, no here. They keep your mind busy & you will waste your mental energy & time thinking about them. Family and kids are the biggest time & mental energy consumers but you cannot avoid them. This is a new world you need mental energy to survive.

Avoid sports gossip, celebrity gossip don't get occupied by it.

I will suggest you some tools which can help you save time and be more productive.

AMAZON ECHO
this is a cool IOT enabled Artificial intelligence device, you just need to say "Alexa" and your command, like "Alexa what time is it". It will tell you current time based on you location, it can also wake you up, Alexa wake me up at 5 am everyday & it will set alarm for you at 5.am every day. You can also ask for information about certain topics, and it will search on the

internet for you and will also read it out for you. You can also ask it to play music; you can ask Alexa to read your kindle eBooks, it can also play audible books, it can also take your shopping orders and can also directly place order, it can be connected to your home devices and you can switch on or off lights at your home.

You see the time saving here, you save ton of time, it will definitely make you lazier.

FREEDCAMP

Coolest thing about freedcamp.com is they give you ton of functionality for free. I **myself** using it. It's a great tool
it lets you manage your team and assign tasks to them. You can discuss with team members.

You can register here
http://www.freedcamp.com

EVERNOTE

ideas occur when you least expect it, mostly ideas occur when you are in bathroom, walking on the road, chatting with friends. The moment you get an idea record it using Evernote, lot of Professionals and

Entrepreneurs doing it.

This is a useful tool, lots of us have a brilliant idea in odd situations and then later we don't even remember it or we don't remember the details at all.

Check out here

https://evernote.com

BUFFER.COM

it lets you manage all the social media accounts, twitter, Facebook, Google+, Pinterest, LinkedIn. You can also schedule posts. If you have followers it is useful for you.

Try here

https://buffer.com/

IFTTT

"if this then that", it is an IOT enabled service, it lets you automate your tasks, it lets you create recipes, like "if it is going to rain tomorrow send me an email" and it will do so.

Try it out
https://ifttt.com

RESCUE TIME
Facebook is the biggest time waster, once you log in, you get busy in seeing videos and pictures shared by your friends, it is highly distractive in nature and won't let you focus, here comes rescue time to save you, it lets you block distractive sites and also let you know which programs or websites you are spending more time, and also which days and hours you were most productive
try it here

https://www.rescuetime.com/

STAYFOCUSED
it is a free Google chrome extension, it restricts your time on time wasting websites like Facebook, it is customizable according to your needs.

One more thing I will like to tell you, is learn keyboard shortcuts that will save you lot of time, avoid procrastination instead try to do work ahead of the time, that will save you time, for example if you do 3 days' work in 1 day, you get 2 days free for yourself. Spend time on things today that will give you more time tomorrow.

THIS BOOK WILL CONSTANTLY BE UPDATED, SO STAY TUNED, ANYTHING NEW COMES UP WE WILL ADD IT

Some of my other books

You can follow my amazon blog

http://www.amazon.com/Amin-B-Nagpure/e/B01BKB9UX0/ref=ntt_dp_epwbk_0

What to follow
keep yourself updated with latest information, I will give some links which you follow and put important information into your brains

Follow me
http://www.aminnagpure.com

Follow TEDX, they are group of geniuses

https://www.youtube.com/user/TEDxTalks

Follow Lazy Ass Stoner

https://www.youtube.com/user/TheLazyAssStoner

www.ingramcontent.com/pod-product-compliance
Lightning Source LLC
LaVergne TN
LVHW022337060326
832902LV00022B/4083